MICROSCOPY OF HAPPY LIVING
"DON'T WORRY-BE POSITIVE"
"START LIVING"

BALDEV BHATIA
A Partridge India
A PENGUIN RANDOM HOUSE COMPANY
(Paper Pack)

MICROSCOPY OF HAPPY LIVING
"DON'T WORRY-BE POSITIVE"
"START LIVING"

BALDEV BHATIA
A Partridge India
A PENGUIN RANDOM HOUSE COMPANY
(Paper Pack)

PARTRIDGE
A Penguin Random House Company

To order additional copies of this book, contact
Partridge India
000 800 10062 62
orders.india@partridgepublishing.com

www.partridgepublishing.com/india

CONTENTS

BLESSING OF GOD GANESHA

WITH THE BLESSING OF MAA SARASWATI

BLESSING OF GOD SHIVA

BLESSING OF GOD SHIVA AND PARVATI

BLESSING OF OMKAR

INTRODUCTION

What do we think about happiness? The feeling of happiness is within us. It is said that happiness is purely an internal matter. It has nothing to do with our external circumstances. There is something positive within us who keep us happy and there is something negative within us which keep you unhappy. Happy living is nothing more than that of living a normal life free from undue pressures, problems and tensions. If we want to live a happy life then we need to get rid of the negative which makes us unhappy. Negative approach always complicates the problems and increases unhappiness. Most of us do the fatal mistake of looking outwards for happiness rather than looking inwards. Be happy and positive every day. Even if we are having a bad day, think of some good things that may come in our way, either later that day, tomorrow, next week, month, or year. When everything seems to be beyond our control, it's almost too easy for us to slip into the grasp of pessimism or negativity. To avoid negativity we must strive to abolish this sort of thinking through the power of thinking positively. The Art of Happy Living is not a complicated kind of art difficult to learn rather a simple art of living well, eating well, thinking well and feeling well. What we need to do is just to tune up our mind to enjoy every moment of life and let the happiness follow us. This is something that needs to be looked into thoroughly. We need to focus on the positive aspects lives, rather than on the negative setbacks. We must remember that happy living is the reward of positive thinking. We ought to remember; only the positive thinking can bring happiness in our lives. If we cannot think positively, you cannot live happily. Be our own teacher or adviser we ought to look everything with a positive angle. Let us find something good even in most critical moments of our life and let us make positive thinking the basis of our happy living. It's a matter of thought that fools worry about the circumstances on which they have no control. Why worry when we cannot change the climate, rather enjoy it whether it's hot, humid, cold, cloudy, foggy or snowy. Let us all keep our internal weather mind body and soul pleasant all the time. Happiness is all around. It's not far away from us. If we do not want to live happy, it's up to us. It's our own choice. We must not blame others, nor should we blame our fate or external circumstances. Another thing is that feeling confident affects the way we perceive our situations and how we decide to manage them. Think that by being more optimistic we alter our approaches to situations and take on them in a healthier manner; we think of alternatives and act according to better outcomes. If we think positive it will be positive. It does not say to stick our heads in the soil; rather it says to think positive. Interestingly it does not say feel positive it says think positive and that is the real meaning to remain happy. Happiness does not come alone it adds our minds body and soul to remain in constant touch with each other. We have to remove negative thoughts and create and atmosphere to be happy in our lives. There are many fear factors that are reasoning us to be unhappy and the main reason being that our heart and our feelings which are more susceptible to fear and worry then the mind. Of course we do the worrying in our minds but it is our emotions that are worried not our brains. When the heart senses the possibility of loss it can start panicking and then uses the mind to worry and many times tries to manipulate the brain in dealing with the fear. The heart desires something and gets excited about it and then it manipulates the mind to assure that it will get it. Although the brain can control the emotions and knowledge precedes all, however when it comes to response time the brain is slower than the emotions. That is which explains why we say or do things and then regret them. Our objective in life should be to train ourselves to wait for the brain to show up before we say or do anything. Fear usually comes from the emotions and thinking positive is something the brain is capable of doing. It would be very hard to tell someone who is worried to feel positive. But if you tell them to think positive that is something even a worried person can do. We need to use our mind to think positive, to think of a positive outcome. Thinking positive brings positive results in its wake; when we react in a positive way to a negative situation we usually get positive in return. Positive mental attitude is effective in many ways. There are limits to the effectiveness of positive thinking. It is not always enough to change deeply entrenched irrational core beliefs about our self, others and the world. When someone does something to us do we think about it in a positive way or in a negative way? Do we try to assume that the person who is not treating us the way we should be treated is in pain himself and needs our love or do we assume that they just don't like us and therefore we need to respond back in that kind? It is therefore a must for us to learn understand and remember that we need to be positive and think positive in the interest of our happy living.

"DON'T WORRY--BE POSITIVE" – "THINK POSITIVE"
AND "START LIVING A HAPPY LIFE"

SD/-
(BALDEV
BHATIA)
AUTHOR

Date: JULY 24TH 2014

17

PREFACE

Author Baldev Bhatia shares with millions of curious readers the 'real knowledge' by letting them know more about themselves in detail about their in born positive qualities, possessed by them and also guides them to ward off the negativity in them, by getting to know as how to live happily. The worries troubling them, the negative forces influencing them, need to be discarded forever for a positive and happy living.

A thought of penning down the wonders of this mystic manuscript has lured the author cum astrologer to bring to the millions of readers the 'real knowledge' by letting them know more about themselves in detail about their inborn positive qualities that they already possess, guiding them how to discard the negativity in them, with the help of astrological science.

This manuscript has been written specially to ward off the negative forces influencing the masses and of the negativity in them. This book gets them to know more about their zodiac signs, their habits, characteristics; appearances; their personality; profession, career; business, finances, their match with other Zodiac signs; romance, marriage, weakness their health and disease and finally the negative forces governing them charming them to become more positive and to lead a happy life. This manuscript reveals a whole lot of information which one is in search for the truths of a positive attitude.

This microscopy of happy living is based on the practical experience of the author who has meet several thousand people having got negativity in their personal lives and those leading a miserable life totally being depressed and dejected. The main object of writing this manuscript is to impart the basic knowledge of how to become bold, courageous, and how to throw away the negative forces and become a positive person in life.

The author has shared the experience of his life with his esteem readers. His published books "Microscopy of Astrology", Microscopy of Numerology", Microscopy of Remedies also guide his readers to achieve their personal goals with ease and assist them to overcome all the problems, crises, and the unforeseen negatives forces, in their lives and guides them not to be disheartened or depressed.

This book goes to reveal, the real facts of life and the destiny as to what is stored for each and every reader in his or her future. Various chapters have been covered and maximum emphasis have been paid to cover the subjects pertaining to the significance of different houses in one's chart; different Zodiac signs, planets and their placements in different houses and signs; affliction of planets with the interpretation of the major period and the meaning of the Birth Signs and also the zodiac compatibility of the individual birth signs.

Author and Astrologer Baldev Bhatia have put his entire life experience in promoting positivity among his clients through the mystic world of the astrology science and other various fields.

He has done so in order to serve millions of curious readers of this mystic science with a good intension of imparting them the real knowledge of how to become a positive person in life. The author-cum astrologer has been associated with general public for the past 45 years and has been practicing psychology and pubic healing. His aim is also to guide the readers to achieve their personal goals with ease and assists them to overcome all the problems, crises, speed breakers and the unforeseen negatives forces, in their lives by not getting disheartened or depressed in their lives.

The author's main message, through this manuscript to his readers is to spread, the message of "LOVE, PEACE AND HAPPINESS" TO THE ENTIRE WORLD AND GUIDES HIS READERS TO WARD OFF "DEPRESSION, DEJECTION HATRED, AND NEGATIVITY IN THEIR LIVES". THE AUTHOR HAS ALSO REVEALED TO HIS READERS TO ATTAIN POSTIVENESS IN THEIR LIVES AND REACH TO THE "PATH OF GLORY BY GETTING AWAY FROM THEIR WEAKNESS OF NEGATIVE THINKING, DEPRESIVE LIFE AND TO LEAD A POSITIVE AND HAPPY LIFE".

The chapters in the book are very useful, purposeful, and a pin point to the service of mankind. He wishes success for all his readers.

The author would definitely like to express his sincere thanks to Ms. Alpa Shah Director, Travel Company of UK, for helping and encouraging him to pen down this book in the interest of Depressed and Dejected and the so called Negative persons of this world.

He is also grateful and thankful to A Partridge India A PENGUIN RANDOM HOUSE COMPANY for publishing his book.

DATED
JULY 24TH 2014

SD/-
BALDEV BHATIA
Author

CHAPTER ONE

DON'T WORRY

- Basic factors of analyzing worry-
What is a worry?

Thought which are provoking our mind, about the uncertainties and the negativities, as to what will happen tomorrow. Worries are repetitive thoughts associated with feelings of anxiety in anticipation of some negative future event. Whether the worries are about financial crisis, family problems, work, health or any topic of concern, the anxious feelings produced and sustained by the imaginary thoughts which always distinctly appear to be unpleasant.

Worrying will carry tomorrow's load with today's strength. Worry will not empty tomorrow of its sorrows, it empties today of its power and strength. Worries make you to move into tomorrow ahead of time. Half the worry in the world is caused by people trying to make decisions before they have sufficient knowledge on which to base a decision.

Why worry about the future. Just imagine as to what if we just acted like everything was easy and there was nothing very serious about it to come in future. Worry often gives a small thing a big shadow and its surrounding do frightened with more scary things.

Why worry about tomorrow; concentrate on today happening as for tomorrow will worry about itself. Each day has its own worries and troubles. If there is not any solution to the some problem then do not waste time worrying about it. And if there is a solution to the problem then why waste time worrying about it.

Worry will never rob tomorrow of its sorrows, but will only deny today of its meaning happiness and joys.

Worrying is actually a form of superstition and creates false images in our mind and that is the main reason and cause which makes and leads us to this point of imagination. A human being can survive almost anything, as long as he or she sees the end in sight.

If something bad or good is to happen it is sure to happen, whether we worry or not. Let us put our energy into today and stop worrying about the future and past. We should not foresee trouble, or worry about what may never happen as past is dead and gone forever and future is uncertain and yet to come.

The basic facts we should know about worry. The basic techniques to analyze worry and how to break the worry habit before it breaks us. These are the simple ways where we can concentrate and get rid of worries prevailing in our thoughts.

Annalise worry to see and get the reasons and facts of worry. To avoid reoccurrence of worries, concentrate on prayers as prayers are the best source of remedies of the prevailing worries. The more you pray, the less you'll panic. The more you worship, the less you worry. There is nothing that wastes the body like worry, and anyone who has any faith in God should need not to worry about anything whatsoever is to happen in future.

We ought to know the basic fundamental of analyzing worries. Worries create unnecessary thoughts and these are caused by people going in for unwanted decisions, fore hand not even knowing as to when a good decision is made and not even having sufficient knowledge about it. We must first study and after carefully weighing all the facts than only come to a powerful decision. Simply making castles in the air won't solve our problems but add more to our vows.

Anxiety and worry can go hand in hand. When anxiety grabs the mind, it is self-perpetuating. Your mind gets clogged with numerous with buts and ifs. Do not worry about your life. Worries are repetitive thoughts associated with feelings of anxiety in anticipation of some negative future event. Yet anxious feelings and the worries that lead to them can prove helpful.

It becomes a difficult problem if you are constantly anxious as it will become a hindrance to your everyday life, rather than motivate you to some good and better things. Never worry alone. Worrisome thoughts reproduce faster so one of the most powerful ways to stop the spiral of worry is simply to disclose the worry to a friend. What you will eat or drink; or about your body, what you will wear.

If you know that the circumstance is beyond your control or power change than revise it to your liking. Just try to put a stop-less order on your worries. Don't permit little things which become insects of life to ruin your happiness. Co-operate with the inevitable. Decide just how much anxiety a thing may be worth and refuse to give in anymore. All the happiness is not given in one go it comes slowly and slowly.

If your worries center around, an important relationship in your life, pay special attention to remain positive and be happy. To keep yourself happy, treat your worried thoughts as valuable signals. How to keep from worrying about criticism?. Simply unjust criticism is often a disguised compliment. It often means that you have aroused jealousy and envy. Let's keep a record of the fool things we have done and criticize ourselves.

The utmost cause of worry is your state of depression. Worries are there to motivate information-gathering and problem-solving. Depression is the inability to construct a future. Depression is inertia. That's the thing about depression: But depression is so insidious, and it compounds daily, that it's impossible to ever see the end. Depressed people think they know themselves, but maybe they only know depression. There are no hopeless than this to get depressed.

Our attitude towards suffering and depression becomes very important because it can affect how we cope with suffering when it arises. Depression is nourished by a lifetime of un grieved and unforgiven causes. Never worry about your heart till it stops beating. How can you deal with anxiety? You might try what when you did. A person worried so much that he decided to hire someone to do his worrying for him. Times will change for the better when you change. Worry is a misuse of the imagination. Worry is most often a prideful way of thinking that you have more control over life and its circumstances than you actually do.

To keep yourself happy, treat your worried thoughts as valuable signals. These are the fundamental facts you should be familiar about worries. A huge factor to stay happy is to cater your worries around, an important relationship in your life and pay special attention sustaining positive relationships. Worries are there to motivate information gathering and problem-solving. Make your mind firm and do come to a positive decision as come what we will not allow the worries to entire our mind and soul.

Once a decision is carefully reached we should get busy carrying out our decisions and should not bother about all the anxieties that are about to come. When we, or any of our colleagues or associates, are about to worry about a problem, we must write it out and think of the following questions: Instead of worrying about what people say of you, why not spend time trying to accomplish something they will admire.

What if we just acted like everything was easy? How would your life be different if you stopped worrying about things we can't control and started focusing on the things we can? Let today be the day. You free yourself from fruitless worry, seize the day and take effective action on things you can change...

CHAPTER TWO

WHAT DO YOU GET OUT OF WORRYING?

You may feel largely uncomfortable, when worries attack your thoughts and mind which makes worrying about a situation an easier option to get depressed and diffused. While you are consuming more worries you are far too busy to do anything else to fix the real problem and would rather find it hard to get into a smart solution. Thus resulting in a fact that you spend your evenings worrying only without even bothering to find some time to search a new job. You get nothing out of worrying except only to think and cry.

Another cause of getting worried is the attachment with which your inner soul gets attracted to. Attachment brings worry. If you have a problem and you come up with the answer, you stop worrying immediately. Our minds can be dishonest, persuading us that we are worrying about something, when our deepest fear is entirely different. No-one likes to admit that they've chosen to worry.

The first step is to write down your worries, which will help you make sense of them, and then decide on one small step you can take towards a solution. But to be very true no man in this world is free of obstacles or difficulties. Don't make worry your habit. Break this habit and stop all the negative and panic thoughts provoking your mind all the time.

If you can't change the past, but you must not ruin the present by worrying about the future. Joy is what happens to us when we allow ourselves to recognize how good things really are. When we feel worried and depressed, we need to consciously form a smile on our faces and act upbeat until the happy feeling becomes genuine reality.

Feelings of depression and hopelessness and or anger are even tougher to cope with on a consistent basis.

When you are worried, you not only hurt yourself, but the limited support systems that are still holding on your mind but making you to get more and more worried and nothing is achieved in terms of success except the re-carnation of worries and worries.......

Your actions breed confidence and courage. If you want to conquer fear, anger and worry do not sit ideal and just think about it. Let our deep worrying become advance thinking and planning. If you look into your own mind and heart, and you find nothing wrong there, what is there to worry about? Practically nothing what is there to fear about and again nothing? So why worry unnecessarily and make your present and future dark.

CHAPTER THREE

REMOVE NEGETAVE THOUGHTS BE POSITIVE

All your thoughts, good and bad, are the creation which tends to lead you to a materialistic life and go in to generate unnecessary worries. That is why you must learn to be more positive. The environment and all the experiences in your life are the results of your habitual and dominant thoughts.

Negative thoughts could tell us about something that needs special attention when they lead us to the path of worries. We must discover what needs to be done, and think positively to take care of it. Many of us fail to see a negative occurrence and do not think of a replacement of negative thought with positive one.

They even do not look for a bright side in every situation. If we do this for a longer period of time, we become habitual, and it will make a tremendous delay in improving our positive thinking skills. We must remember, everything can be framed positively if we make a restless effort to do so.

There are both positive and negative aspects to most situations. We get to choose which ones we will focus on. We can try to catch ourselves when we're being negative and do not try thinking the opposite.

There's no sense in worrying about the negatives if these negatives cannot be changed. If we waste energy and happiness on the things we can't change, we'll only make ourselves more frustrated and come to the stage of depression.

Negativity is a habit and we often don't realize we're doing ourselves down. Under each negative thought you've written, see if you can spot an alternative way of looking at it, that isn't so negative.

There's a world of difference between expecting failure or rejection - so as not to be disappointed when it occurs - and recognizing it as a possibility. It's sensible to look at a situation from all angles and to have a back-up plan to fall back on if need be. People who do this will often see failure as another step on the road to eventual success; but by expecting and envisioning success, there's less likely to be a failure.

Let us find some ways of removing negative thoughts and discouraging our worries to be born.

1. By way of giving a good Smile

The first easiest way is smiling. Many theories have revealed that even a forced smile can lift one's mood. We may also share positivity with others by flashing them with a brilliant smile. Smiling is a reward, not a risk. The only thing we risk when smiling is a giving ourselves a little more happiness.

2. By way of having the company of good friends.

Keep yourself busy and surround yourself with good friends. Appreciate the people in your life who have stood by you through thick and thin. Count their support which has helped you become more positive, and in the process you will probably help them too. Good friends help each other in the days of crises and through both the good and bad times. Feel positive about them and feel lucky to have them in your company.

3. Focus your thoughts on positive imagination

Focus your imagination and make efforts on becoming that new positive person. It is much easier to bring about change if you just put your mind to it and change your thoughts into a much more positive direction. We know that it is difficult for us to control things that happen in our lives, but we can, with some effort, control what we think or do in our lives. Positive thinking will make our imagination livelier and we would be able to lead our lives without many worries. Depression, however, has consequences that could ruin your self-esteem, health, and well-being.

CHAPTER FOUR

CREATE LIFE WITHIN YOU.

If you are interested in getting more success, focus on all the ways as if you have already attained success. You need to focus on the thing and create a live within you. If you want love and affection, focus on all the people and the abundance of love that you have to give to them. If we want to have greater health, focus on all the ways that we are healthy, thus creating and delivering a good life within you.

You need to admit that there are problems that you cannot change. But you can change the way of your thinking if you identify the main reason of the problem. And if you acknowledge the facts, that you have been negative or inactive in finding a solution to the problem, probably this will make it easier for you to become positive thus creating a new lease of life within you.

You must try to make goals. Making goals can give you a more positive outlook on life. People often tend to get bored with life and get the feeling that they are stuck to negative things which the result they often get the feeling of being depressed. Setting a direction for yourself and a goal would surely help you to move forward. If you expecting to succeed, and are not afraid of failure, you have the best chance of staying positive and can create a very positive life within you. When you, or any of your associates, are tempted to worry about a problem, write out the solution and a definite answer to it. This helps a positive feeling to generate within you.

Another thing you need to understand is that there are several ways to cultivate a mental attitude that can bring you peace and happiness and can carnage a good life within you. More of it if you fill your mind with thoughts of peace, courage, health, and hope, your life will be easy to live. You would get a happy feeling of life and mind If you let yourself to forget your own unhappiness, by trying to create a little happiness for others. You are best to yourself. The perfect way to conquer worry is the Prayer of God. To keep yourself from worrying about criticism, do not even try to get mixed with your enemies, because if you do you will hurt yourself far more than we hurting them. Instead of worrying about ingratitude, let's expect it. Let's remember that the only way to find happiness is not to expect gratitude, but to give for the joy of giving. Let us build a happy life within us....generate peace and a healthy atmosphere around us. This will help us to lead a peaceful happy and prosperous life and we would find ourselves to be happier than before. You should do things in the order of their importance.

You need to clear your desk of all papers except those relating to the immediate problem at hand. When you face a problem, solve it then and there, if you have the facts to make a decision. Make a decision fast and do not linger on. Learn to organize, deputize, and supervise and straight away come to decision. Simply postponing it would spoil your good thoughts and there is every likelihood your mind may get into negative activities and start thinking in negative manner. Therefore write down a list of things that make you excited, however big, small, likely or unlikely. Then work to make them occur more often. Look for moments of joy and savor them. Recognize your good happening every day.

Take care of your health

Eat well do plenty of exercise and do not skip meals It is a known fact that Physical exercise is known to stimulate our veins and get to strengthen our minds that lift depression and anxiety so we need to walk, swim, run or whatever we like doing best. Those who create or those who do well on the worst scenario, give themselves worry and stress, tend to be devastated.

If we cannot get some sunshine, we can always lighten up our rooms with brighter lights. We can have lunch outside the office. Take frequent walks instead of driving our cars over short distances. No man is indispensable.

First of all our circle of friends is always there to give us some moral support. Spending time and engaging ourselves in worthwhile activities could give us a very enjoyable and satisfying feeling. Nothing feels better than having group support. Good friends are quite important and their company generally lightened up our spirits. To get to know and to find such friends we simply have to be friendly with ourselves, and then the friendships will naturally follow us.

We need to understand the power of touch and support and we have not to underestimate it strength and support. Don't we feel so good when someone pats us on our back and gives us some words of encouragement during your most challenging times and difficult times. Just hug or embrace someone someday you will see that you have almost changed his life. Get intimate with him and try to establish close ties with his family and friends. The love and care expressed by you will tremendously boost him and well as your immune system and fury of worry will be diminished for all.

In our lives storms may come and go in the form of reversals, but if we have the power and foundation of inner fulfillment and if we deal with it with a very clear practical mind these storms will not kill us or will not disrupt us. There could be numberless reasons for which we keep on worrying. We may be worried about our health, wealth, loved ones, friends, the happening f yesterday and the follow happenings of tomorrow, the environment or the world politics, but these can be dealt with firm mind and fearless worry if we generate within ourselves the power of enlightenment within ourselves.

CHAPTER FIVE

HAPPINESS IS A STATE OF MIND.

Happiness is something you cannot earn or buy. If you have spent your life trying to get some happiness or something that will make you happy, odds are that you are wasting a really good life that you don't know you have. You passed up and overlooked a lot of personal happiness. You are probably spending so much time chasing and dreaming of unnecessary thing of what could be of no use to you and that you are forgetting about all the small and big things occurring right now that could make you happy. People and things alone, won't make you happy. Your own efforts not to get worried or depressed make you happy. You know the saying, that "Happiness is a state of mind". And state of mind is what you think do and act in a peaceful manner without being getting worried or depressed.

The best thing about happiness is that you get it is free. You don't have to pay or you do not have to open any account to be happy. You don't have to pay monthly rent for it either. You just have to change your perspective, your views on what you are seeing and feeling. Happiness is not something which is quite readymade. It comes from your own actions and deeds. Don't let one cloud darken the whole sky. Angriness and happiness don't mix. You must dig out the angriness in you, and see that the happiness has shown and seeded a place to grow its roots.

The ultimate goal of life should be to get happiness and not get involved into unnecessary worries falling in the death trap of defeats and failures. The essence of life is not in the great victories and grand failures, but in the simple joys. The purpose of our lives is to be happy. Laugh when you can, apologize when you should, and let go of what you can't change. Think positive and just visualize that what is stored in destiny would not be negative. If you want to be happy, practice meditation. If you want, others to be happy practice compassion.

Whoever is happy will make others happy, too. Let us be very sure and let us keep in mind that happiness doesn't depend on any superficial conditions, it is governed by our mental attitude only. Our greatest gift to others is to be happy and to radiate our happiness to the entire world. Happiness is a guide to direction, not a place to hide. As a happy person, you radiate happiness to the world. Visualize your light radiating throughout the world, passing from person to person until it encircles the globe. Resolve to keep happy, and your joy and you shall form an invincible host against difficulties.

The positive persons often dance to the happy tunes of their lives. The path to happiness is forgiveness of everyone and gratitude for everything. Happiness fills your heart each day and your whole life through with clean thoughts. Any day would be a wonderful day if you do not to take life so seriously. Happiness is not about being a winner -it's about being gentle with life being gentle within you. Happiness blooms in the presence of self-respect and the absence of ego. Love yourself. Love everyone around you. Love everyone in the whole world.

When you're feeling depressed or anxious, close your eyes and try to visualize a guided positive imaginary thing. First breathe deeply and relax. How important it is to consistently reach for positive, uplifting, inspirational thoughts. Thought that promote aliveness and abundance. Thoughts that make you feel good. Look at the birds of the air; they do not sow or reap or store away in barns, and yet our heavenly Father feeds them. Imagine that you're already a positive person and you love life. The only thing between us and our desire, to be happy, is one single fact: we are not happy because we often fall into the death trap of depression and wholly because of our negative thoughts. Absence of positive thinking, has eluded us of our great happiness and left us far behind. This very little known fact has kept many of us from reaching our goal of happiness. If you keep thinking things like as if your life is dead!", nothing would be achieved and it will be like that only. Throw away all your negative thoughts and worries, concentrate on the goals to be achieved, on the ray of happiness in you and make sure that you are not falling again into the path of negativity. "Happiness is a state of mind only and not the thoughts of negatives"....

CHAPTER SIX

HAPPINESS AND POSTIVENESS

You may also feel that life has become terrible for you to live and you are carrying no hope that someone would be there to rescue you. Happiness is your own choice and decision. Each of us can be as happy as we make up our minds to be. We can, if we want, fill up our days with positive attitude chatter and laughter. To be happy, we need to concentrate only on happy thoughts. The ghosts of the past have to be exorcised. You may be working in any field, the key to success is your outlook. Sometimes you may think that no road is left for you from where you can achieve the happiness of life. There may be chances that someone who was there with you before might hold on to you when you are on the dark side of the life.

The experience has taught us that we should buy some strength, hope and positive ness from our loved ones to help ourselves in such a situation rather than surrendering as life is a precious gift of God and is equipped with full of joy and happiness if we help ourselves in these critical moments and live with considerable optimism. Happiness in life comes through the doors of positive thoughts; we do not even realize which one is left open. We have so many reasons to cry and at the same time plenty of reasons to smile as well.

Keeping our dreams and hope alive might be a reason that success and happiness will come our way again. We ought to know that happiness alone does not stand for anything, but it is on our way of thinking that how do we keep ourselves happy in life. Ending up our lives does not lead us to our destination but of course proves we are supposed to be cowards who know not to unfold the doors of belief in God and in ourselves. Failure and disappointment are part of our life. The only thing is that we need to face and solve the problem. We must not forget to believe in God whatever our situation may be, we would be taken away from Him by the difficulties, in order that we bow down and surrender.

But if our faith is strong enough we will not be let down, rather we would break the knees of sorrows and force it to die and lead happy lives. We should not surrender but must find out ways to come out of our worries, anxieties and difficulties. We ought not to indulge ourselves into the darkness of the room but find out the doors to free ourselves from unnecessary fear and worries. We must belief in ourselves and our hearts, and believe in the ones who love us and not the ones whom we love. We must not fall on the negative side of a thing. It is the real time when you keep on revealing the truth of our lives and relations, do not fall on the reverse side but think how good it was that because of the hard times of our lives we could well judge about them. We should always try to be positive and should think that whatever is happening, it is the positive side or consequence of that incident in would be on the positive side of our imagination. With all these thoughts, I would request my readers to implement some good thoughts in their life that would make things easier to be tackled by them. We should accept the situation and fight it with more determination.

In this world nothing is good or bad and only thinking makes it so. We ought to know that advice from people around us will help us to overcome from the any drastic situation. Also we have to always minimize the stress as it gives nothing but takes away joy and happiness from our lives. And finally we need to take things casually and fight with it seriously. The next morning after all, will surely come with fresh air to breathe the new hopes in us with the brightness of the sun. A clear minded person looks for good qualities in the other person, whereas a negative mind always looks for the fault in the other person, whereas a negative mind always looks for the fault. An optimist goes forward keeping in mind the past, a pessimist thinks of the future and reverts back to the past. In fact negative thoughts are our greatest enemies. Experience the happiness in all circumstances by maintaining better relationships.

How about understanding that sadness cannot touch a person with a positive attitude? The capability increases as It boosts up patience and confidence. It increases the decision of making power. Creative way of thoughts appears in the mind. Positive thoughts teach the art of finding solutions to any problem. Optimism is something what we do. Anxiety and other negative emotions are known to be detrimental to the body, especially to our immune systems, and having an optimistic nature seems to protect against those effects. People who are supposed to be optimistic, about their future, behaving differently. They do exercise, do not indulge in in smoking and often follow a good and better diet. Whenever we are unhappy, if we analyze the reason for our unhappiness, it is because life is not matching our expectations.

CHAPTER SEVEN

STOP WORRYING, BE POSITIVE AND START LIVING HAPPILY

Is it true that do you constantly worry about what people think of you?. If yes, then you need to follow these tips to get over your worries:

1. Tip No 1

Realization:

We need to know and realize that nobody is perfect or flawless. If we try to change the way we look, talk and behave just to please others, and show our pride we will gradually become such a person that we ourselves won't recognize each other and would start and create unnecessary worries within us and our surrounding without being positive and will not start to live happily. We ought to stop worrying over unnecessary things be positive and live without fear happily.

2. Tip No 2

Recognition:

We need to understand that what people think of us is their concern, and not ours. If they think about us to be, too reticent or proud, it's really not our business. If every time we happen to meet some new fellows, we may wonder and imagine as what they think of us, and with this feeling in us we will never be able to live a trouble-free and hassle free life. We are bound to fall into the trap of unnecessary worries denying us the startup of new and the happy living life.

3. Tip No.3

Rationalization:

We must think rationally. Is it in our hands or can we control what others think about us?. Simply we need to ignore them If we cannot, and live our lives the way we want to and find the ways to leave worries aside and start living a happy life. Let us make our way to happy living.

4. Tip No 4

Positive Thinking with Positive Attitudes.

It is a well-known fact that attitude decides how a natives or persons copes up with the day to day events of life. Attitude is what a influence a person's reaction to a situation in life is. It sets the emotional undertone for a person to his likes or dislikes a situation even before he is acquainted with it. Positive attitude is a quality that is second to none in a human being.

We acknowledge our children to say a big thank you from the time to time irrespective they being very little, we teach them to be grateful for everything that they receive. We attach so much importance to this attitude of gratitude that when our children fail to thank someone, we insist that they do it. That is what is needed to be avoided from time to time. We expect this in return from others when we help them or give them a gift. We call a person discourteous and rude when they do not say thank us in return. Though we attach so much importance to this attitude, as we grow into teenage and adult years we find ourselves becoming ungrateful or taking things for granted. We lose touch with the very same qualities that we instill in our children. We take for granted our life, our health, our families, the people in our lives, the things that our loved ones do for us to make our lives easier and things that we possess.

The attitude of positive speaks a lot about a person. It denotes about changing negative attitudes and making positive thinking a positive attitude a good habit. Thinking positively and a positive attitude help us to appreciate and value ourselves, our potential and all that we have. It ensures that we do not take our abilities for granted. It makes us look at ourselves as special people with a special set of abilities and potential. It banishes the feelings of inadequacy and insecurity that arises from unfair comparisons with others. It helps us to appreciate people for who they are and not magnify what they are not and their little flaws. It drives away prejudice and makes us approach life with an open mind. It predisposes us to react to the daily events of life in a positive manner and help us to look at the brighter side of life. Make us optimistic. It gives hope and helps us look forward to life with anticipation.

We need to know that positive thinking takes the focus away from what we don't have, to appreciating and making good use of what we have. It is closely connected to our emotional wellbeing and happiness. We feel loved and at peace with ourselves for a major part of our lives when we make this attitude ours. This adds and helps us to get rid of greed, amenity, bitterness, jealousy, and promotes a healthy and nurturing attitude towards others, which in turn gets reciprocated and we feel the sense of healthy living.

On the face of it we ought to know that a positive is not an attitude of being satisfied and content, that you never want to do anything, anymore. This is an attitude that makes you feel good about who you are, what you do, and what your potentials are. This attitude impels you to utilize all that you are endowed with as a person, to achieve the highest possible goals. When we have this attitude, we are able to work without any external pressure to perform but there is sufficient pressure and motivation from within.

The possessing of positive thinking is like any other habit, so we need to follow the routine of habit formation here as well. You will win new friends and admirers without having to impress them or conform to the pressure of doing things their way. You will be bubbling with life and the joie de vivre. You will be rearing to go and accomplish all you can with your new found confidence. The best part of adopting the 'positive thinking and a positive attitude of gratitude is that, you will be able to enjoy the smallest pleasures of nature with a heightened sense of satisfaction and awe. I can see and watch a beautiful flower and carry that joy in my mind for future enjoyment with a clear positive habit. I can go back to work freshen and can use it as an object to meditate on when I feel stressed.

Let us be clear that a positive is not an attitude of being satisfied and content, that you never want to do anything, anymore. This is an attitude that makes you feel good about who you are, what you do, and what your potentials are. This attitude impels you to utilize all that you are endowed with as a person, to achieve the highest possible goals. When we have this attitude, we are able to work without any external pressure to perform but there is sufficient pressure and motivation from within. The habit of positive thinking is like any other habit, so we need to follow the routine of habit formation here as well.

CHAPTER EIGHT

FAILURE AND DISAPPOINTMENT SUN SHINE OF NEW HOPES

At time we may think that there is no road is left for us from where we can achieve the happiness of our lives. We may also feel that life has become terrible for us to live and we are carrying new hope that someone would come to rescue us. There may be chances that someone who was there with us before might have held on to us when we were on the dark side of the life.

We should not forget that happiness in life comes through the doors of positive thoughts; we need to have them first. If one door happen to close, another opens, in the event only when we are confident and optimistic. We have so many reasons to cry and at the same time plenty of reasons to smile as well. Similarly, happiness does not stand for anything, but is on our way of thinking that how do we keep ourselves happy in life. Failure and disappointment are part of our life. The only thing is that we need to face and solve the problem is by keeping our dreams and hope alive be it a reason that success and happiness will come our way again.

The experience has taught us that we should buy some strength, hope and positivity from our loved ones to help ourselves in such a situation rather than surrendering as life is a precious gift of God and is equipped with full of joy and happiness if we help ourselves in these critical moments we can live with considerable optimism.

What if when everything goes wrong and all the doors of happiness are closed our live becomes a silent. It is a quite common and we are aware of a marvelous proverb that Life itself is a stage and we all are the performers, performing different acts assigned to us by our almighty power. We should not forget as to what is in our possession?, if it is to fulfill our duties towards our responsibility and do whatever is correct and is allowed by us in our life?. However, despite of all these good thoughts which are embodied to us by the almighty fail to revive these unwanted circumstances that lead us to sorrow and difficulties and a situation where we do not know what is correct and good for us and what is wrong for us.

We should always remember that, "Life is there, where there is hope". That single thing that remains in our hands is to find out ways to know how to overcome these worries of our life at that very moment when all doors are closed for us which means that whatever situation is there, we must not give up hope. We must fight because there have been always a chance that with good faith and hard work we can turn the odds in our favor. It is often said that it is very easy to advise but when it comes to us, things go out of our control and we fail to suggest a way out for ourselves. We fall into the trap of unnecessary worries and elope ourselves with negative thoughts. We feel better when somebody else is facing some difficulty but when it comes to us we fail to gather that faith, will power and the words of strength.

It is a common fact that no one in this world is free of obstacles or difficulties. If all the openings of happiness are shut for us and we have to overcome that and have no way to come out, but to survive lest we must have to learn to swim out of the sorrows because this is what is called life and sorrow free living. There are lot more examples and in many other situations, where we will find that how we could have faced and fought with our sorrows and difficulties of life when there was no hope left in our lives.

When the power of will is at the worst and each one of us knows that the one who is gone never comes back. Neither a thousands of words would not be enough to bring him back nor a million tears, because each and every moment, eyes would only shed tears, mind would remain tensed and we would be simply surrounded by worries and the life seems to have been vanished. Life is ever expanding, contraction is death. As commonly said by big saints that the self- seeking man who is looking after his personal comforts and leading a lazy life for himself there would be no room for him even in the hell and he simply have lost the power of his will.

We are quite aware of the fact that faith in oneself is the history of a man and that faith calls the quality of superiority within a person. One cannot do anything without it. We fail only when we do not try very hard to achieve the power and faith within us. As soon as we lose faith, death comes in our way and we are surrounds by all the evils and stupid worries of the world.

The secret and history of every successful man is to have, good confidence, faith and strength behind him and that remain the right cause of his single success in life. Unselfishness plays a very vital role in his life. He may not have been perfectly unselfish, yet he was tending towards it. If he had been perfectly unselfish, he would have been as great a success. The degree of unselfishness marks the degree of success everywhere and he leads to be successful man without fear worries and selfishness.

There are quite a number of reasons to believe that for a successful and happy life the mystery surrounding it lies in our interests, and good memory which is the basis of our interest, power of desire and aim, keeping ourselves smiling and the doubt free character which is the foremost important reason for a successful and happy life. If we possess one solid unselfish and doubt free character within ourselves we would be quite happy and successful.

The love for God and worshipping God adds to one common thing the immense faith in Him. There may be different beliefs and ways to worship God in different communities, places and religions, but one thing remains the same and that is the Love of God for all of us. Our world is full of odds and evens, happiness and sorrows, fulfilment and emptiness. And these are all created by the Almighty. However, the most beautiful Gift of God, is Human, which is such a mystery driven by Him which could hardly be defined or explained in depth.

We know that life cannot be foreseen. Life is not a bed of roses. Life is a battle field and not a bed of roses as every man on earth has to struggle very hard in making his life happy. If aim of our life is to stay happy and let others to be happy, we will be happy and remembered by all. But no one will actually remember us for the wealth we have gained, or success we have achieved. I have no aim in life. Summary living with no purpose in life is just like a feather moving towards the wind. Both career and purpose are different issues but it is equally important to understand the value of these things which would ultimately add spicy flavor to your living.

Innovation at work place is what is it necessary how well we judge our work, how good we like and enjoy it. If we take our work as a stiff challenge and as learning everyday then we would start loving it and giving our best. However, if we just work for the sake of then nothing is realized and we do not remain happy in life.

Life is such a special gift of Almighty and it is not gifted by Him to use it the way we like or love to. The actual path shown by Him needs to be followed by us for us to reach the peak of betterment every moment. We need to have some positive attitude to look at it comfortably but at the same time having a positive mental attitude does not mean banishing all negative thoughts and people from your life. The same is true with thoughts. When we go to field with negative thoughts, we banish one and another one arises. Therefore creation of positivity in life is utmost necessary to enjoy the special gift of God to us.

Now let's us imagine that we are not feeling at our best today, and we are having thoughts that could be classified as negative. We shouldn't be thinking such negative thoughts. We don't like the negative thoughts. We ought to know that negative thoughts are stressful, demoralizing and depressing. We shouldn't aim to have negative thoughts at all. Often we feel uncomfortable because we think we have to say or do something in response to another person's words. When we find ourselves thinking this way, it helps enormously to take a few moments to check inside and notice what we are feeling. We are deeply depressed that negativity has governed us and has taken a deep root in our minds.....

CHAPTER NINE

STEPS FOR A
SUCCESSFUL AND HAPPY LIFE

The secret of successful and happy life lies in keeping ourselves smiling and the character which is the foremost important reason that lies within us. Do not be curious about anything, but in everything, by prayer and petition, with thanksgiving, present your requests to God. Whenever your mind is tempted to jump the fence and start to worry, say this verse aloud or to yourself. You may even have to repeat it over and over again. Am I constantly striving to see the positive in every aspect of my life?. Steps for a successful and happylife.

Step One:

We need to believe that a Positive Attitude is a choice. This step is hard to take. People are either positive or negative. They tend to blame their negativity on all kinds of outside forces—fate, experiences, parents, relationship, but never really stopped to think that they could choose to be positive. Piercing ourselves that positivity is a choice has been one of the greatest things we have ever done for ourselves. Now when we find ourselves in a bad situation, we know that it's up to us to find the good, to be positive regardless of what's happening around us. We should no longer point fingers and place blame to anyone else. We need to realize that everything happens how it happens, and it's up to us to choose how we want to feel about it. We need to be in control of our attitude, and no one can take that away this from us.

Step Two: Get Rid Your Life of Negativity

If we want to live a positive, joyful life, we must not be surrounded by negative people who don't encourage our happiness. As a negative person, we ought to get attracted too negative people only. Only when we decide to make the change to live a more positive life, we have to get rid of our lives of the most negative influences in it. We are quite aware of the fact that no one is perfect and perfection isn't the goal when it comes to positivity but there were people in our lives who were consistently negative, who constantly bring us down, we need to stop spending so much time with them.

We can very well imagine, it is not easy for us to get away from these negative people. It can hurt us to keep distance from people even when you know they aren't good for us and for our current lifestyle. In addition to removing negative influences from them, we also have to get rid of some of our own negative behaviors, such as the drug and alcohol abuse. We need to take some concrete steps and examine which behaviors are good for us and which were not harmful. What we need is to learn to focus on the positive things, such as working on positive activities and cultivating new, positive relationships. We must let go of the negative ones. This process may be not easy to live a positive life when negative people and behaviors continually pull us down.

Step Three: Look For the Positive in Life

In every situation or in every person there is something good. Most of the time it's not easy to find the positive qualities but we have to look hard to discover positivity in them. Now, when we are faced with a difficult or challenging situation, we need to think and talk to ourselves and console our mind, no matter how terrible the situation might seem, we can always find something good if we take the time to think about it. It is quite obvious that anything good and bad is learning experience so, at the very least, we must learn from bad experiences. However, there's usually even more to it than that. If you really take some time to have a look at it, we would find something good, something genuinely positive, about every person or situation.

Step Four: Reinforce Positivity in Yourself

Once we start thinking more positively, we will realize that we had to reinforce these thoughts and behaviors within ourselves so that we could stick to it. As with any sort of training, the more we practice, the better we get to be positive. The best and easiest way to do this is to be positive when it comes to who we are. We need to speak to ourselves that we are awesome. And we have done a good job at work thus creating positivity within us. We need to be honest with ourselves, and we need to do our best to look for the good. And, whatever we do, we must not focus on the negative. It is alright not to like everything about ourselves, but don't focus on what we don't like. We have all the positive attributes, and it's up to us to remind ourselves of them every day.

Step Five: Share Positivity with Others

Not only do we need to be positive with ourselves for this multiple action to take effect, but we need to be more positive with others. We have to share our wealth of positivity with the people of the world. The best way is to be nice with other people, no matter what. Tell them that they look nice today. Appreciate their job and tell them that have done a great job on that assignment. Be positive and tell your elder or your kids how much you love them and how great they are. When someone is feeling down, do what we need to do is to cheer him or her up. Do send them gifts nice flower and glow them with nice notes.

What is required is that we never wanted to see the good in ourselves and, therefore, didn't want to see it in others also. We must not be critical and condescending rather we must be encouraging and supportive. We should not try to treat others as we would like to be treated, but also try to consider how we would like to be treated. The world likes to appreciate positivity, and the more we share it with others, the more we would be practicing it your own lives. When we start feeling like the idea of not being a positive person we need to remind ourselves that all it takes is one tiny step in the right direction to move towards a more positive attitude. We have to believe in ourselves and remember the most important lesson of all is a positive outlook and that is a choice that we can always make. The power of remaining positive, whatever the situation, can never be underestimated. We are all here for a short duration, but is it worth it to spend any of that time in a any angry or being negative?. That need to sort out in mind and soul and thus must share our positive thoughts with others.

The real test of any one is to remain positive whenever some challenges become difficult. Remaining positive keeps our mind in the right state of balance and often opens resolutions to the problems at hand. Negativity is contagious and spreads like fire. It not only does its affect anyone, but it spreads to everyone who ever comes in contact with it or whoever they interact with. When only the negative perspective is in focus, the resolution process is impeded. Eliminating negativity, or rather, being positive is a mindset that can be found at any moment, and which can be turned into a habit. We must throw away the negativity in us and opt for being a very positive person.

CHAPTER TEN

SHIFT YOUR THOUGHTS

We need to learn a lesson from every situation. No matter how difficult the situation may appear. We should recognize the beautiful lessons waiting to be discovered. Sometimes lessons may prove to be expensive and costly, but every problem is a learning experience in disguise. We need to be conscious of our thoughts, especially, when life just isn't going our way. The moment we see that we are diving into frustration, agony, sorrow or low self –esteem we must shift our thoughts, by thinking about something completely different and unrelated. This will strangle the pattern of self-pity, mind-created imaginations, and negative downward stairs. Really what makes us different from other mammals is our ability to control our thoughts and think for ourselves positively and shift our negative thoughts to a positive angle. We may have made mistakes, but now we can accept it and continue, knowing that we will make a different decision in the future. If we understand this it can be appreciative for the experience. We cannot be both angry and grateful at the same time. We should start counting the blessings and miracles in our lives and if we start exploring for them and we would find more. We should console our mind as to what's not there to be grateful?. It's quite true that we are alive and breathing! We have to realize how lucky we are with all the positivity in abundance in our lives. Our mind and body becomes dumb and mum when it comes to pressure, all it wants to do is take the easiest way out and to throw out of us our negative within us.

Feeling good about ourselves and showing self-confidence boosts our skills potential and capabilities in any areas of work and supports us to become more positive. We need to shift our thoughts from being a negative person to more strong a positive man. Also keeping in mind that pushing things to the limit and going beyond what we think is possible for us to get to the next step of being positive. It becomes another key to achieving what we really want to do.

Even if it may even be relationships and we are finding it difficult to meet someone where we are actually interested in, we need not wait because it usually doesn't come to us by own, we must stand up to get help from any learned fellow. One of the most important things while doing all of this is to be happy about what we are doing, thus we ought to have a successful goal setting our lifestyle with a positive attitude. At times we may suffer from chronic depression, though we know how good things look on to others life cannot be worse for us. Let's imagine how to deal when life leaves a great big steaming pile at our doorstep. Lest we need to remember that external factors can be dealt with by taking positive steps to repair or at least address the root of the problem as best as we can. Whatever may be the primary cause of the problem, that cause must be examined first?.

We may or may not be able to solve the problem, per se, but at least knowing that we are taking positive steps can help us improve our outlook. It will not be easy, of course, for us and it may be like suffering a chronic disease thus we must balance ourselves as "being positive" with an understanding that the reality is, it's going to be an ongoing battle for our own survival. Depression will undermine even the strongest of wills, need help to maintain or at least be reminded of a positive outlook.

Counseling, psychotherapy, and the right combination of medication will play a crucial role in helping to keep us from sinking into that very dark place that is the essence of depression. Be patient, but don't look for miracles. It may be that we will need the help of professionals throughout our lives to maintain a generally even keel. If one could "will away" depression, there would be no need of doctors or drugs. What we can do is understand why we feel like we do, and explain to our counselors that we wish it were that easy, and that we appreciate our concern towards positivity. Shifting our thoughts enables us to the right path of our positivity and thinking in its direction of positivity can make us to lead a very happy life.

CHAPTER ELEVEN

EAT WELL

We need to remember that as we possibly as we can we should make it a point to eat a more balanced, and healthy diet even though we may very little money left with us. We have intake of lot of greens vegetables and with variety of fruit and nuts which are all super healthy food for us and which are more less expensive than meats, cheeses, and processed foods! Their nitrifying value will energize and elevate our body, and knowing this that we are treating ourselves will surely refresh our minds. If we look for rich food rich in vitamins and other useful ingredients which include nuts, soya beans and fatty fish we would get more nutrition value. We must cut back on the caffeine drinks, alcohol. We don't have to quit, but reducing the intake of them will help reduce anxiety and stress from time to time.

The other refreshing factor is naturally our sleep. We need not be reminded of this. Our body is probably begging us for it when we are in the middle of hard times. We may be drawn to maintain good sleeping habits. Maintain a consistent sleep schedule. If we sleep peacefully and our body gets about 8 hours of sleep we get the best results. If we are just starting to have those negative thoughts, we need to speak to the physician or the therapist. They would prescribe us something to help us back to the center, emotionally. Leave that call to the professionals.

Having goals which are set again and again after each one is achieved will give us a mindset or target to strive for which leads to success, with success becomes natural positive attitude. With all positive attitudes, aims and goals success builds a higher potential and belief within us. Setting realistic goals and by staying positive will give us as we know a great beginning to success.

Being positive instead of negative makes an excellent first impression on anybody. Our attitude around your friends, family and public people really tells them who we are. Positive attitude means to be an absolute, clear-cut, definite, forward-looking and expressively firm with a decision. Having a positive attitude toward something means we are willing to commit and do the work without complaint, which leads to our goals. If we realize that whatever appears negative today will change tomorrow and nothing remains the same. Whether we are positive or negative, the situation will definitely change. So we need to set our minds to be positive. With the habit of remaining positive in all situations takes a commitment to us to take control of our habits. But start small, start paying attention to your emotions, start by wanting to change and always to remain positive.

Communication is ideal for us

If we have a problem or if we happen to face any problem the best thing to do for us is to communicate and find out the information we need and get the full picture, so that the solution becomes apparent and easy. If we are upset, we need to communicate and say how we feel. If anyone does something wrong, again we need to communicate with him. The nature of this universe is that we have to face death, birth, old age, and disease. Everything changes. The biggest problem is that we want to control our environment and be worried all the time for all petty things which are even beyond our control.

SMILING IS THE BEST MEDICINE

Modern thesis and studies have shown that smiling makes natural body chemicals to increase our good health. We receive the same benefits whenever we feel like smiling. Smiling also benefits everyone that sees it. Smiling at others makes them feel good too. So we must smile, it is good for us and good for our recipient.

LAUGHTER BOOSTS US

Laughter boots us. It is also one of the best medicines. Based on the same concept of smiling, laughing burns calories, increases our adrenaline and boosts our health. There are even groups of people who get together just to laugh together and enjoy their spirits and to boost them. They are do not laugh at jokes, they simply laugh for a good health. As of smiling, we do not need to laugh at real things; we just need to do the physical laughing for all of the health benefits.

EXERCISE IS OUR ANOTHER STIMULATOR

Exercise is one of health sport that our body needs most. Be it yoga, cross training, or even a simple walking in the park. This helps keeping our body active and will also help to grow our outlook. If we make it hobby we would enjoy the most. Whether its art, photography, music focusing on something other than the worry factor it will give our mind some good atmosphere to breathe off and would generate a good behavior within us.

Even with small amount of exercise make us feel better. Whenever we feel bluesy, angry or think we may be slipping into negative thinking. Get up to do your blood pumping by doing bit of exercise moving your body here and there which will empowers us to do what we need to do and to do what's right. We need to set a schedule of regular exercise at least 4 days a week for at least 15minutes each session for better health. Even a little bit of this exercise will help us, generate good thoughts and ward off the negativity in us. We may start out in small, which will be quite good and fine, simply by doing exercise for ten minutes a day and slowly increase it.

LET US ROLL IT OFF US BACK –

We need not hold on to anything that bothers our mind. It would only hurt our health and it won't help overcome our problems at all. The people who do not hold grudges nor hold on to negative feeling tend to live the longest in this world. We have to visualize our worries on a large chalkboard in our minds. Watching would take ourselves to wider depth and would be a big eraser and would erase our problems. Every time the thoughts come back into our heads, we need to see ourselves with the eraser again. We must keep our slate clean! We ought to remember that worry does not empty tomorrow of its sorrow, it empties today of its strength. Let us be clear that if a problem is fixable one and, if a situation is such that you can do something about it, then there is no need to worry. If it's not fixable, then there is no help in worrying. There is no benefit in worrying whatsoever.." Life is what we make it, so make it a happy one!! Don't worry on things that may not happen, life is too short to worry too much. Smile and be happy.

Therefore do not worry about tomorrow, for tomorrow will worry about itself. Each day has enough trouble of its own. Do not anticipate trouble, or worry about what may never happen. Keep in the sunlight. Imagine every day to be the last of a life surrounded with hopes, cares, anger and fear. The hours that come unexpectedly will be much the more grateful. The mind that is anxious about future events is miserable. Present fears are less than horrible imaginings. Let us be of good cheer, remembering that the misfortunes hardest to bear are those that never happen, focus on the positive aspects of their lives, rather than on the negative setbacks. Feeling confident affects the way we perceive our situations and how we decide to manage them.

Don't waste your life in doubts and fears: spend yourself on the work before you, well assured that the right performance of this hour's duties will be the best preparation for the hours or ages that follow it. It is not work that kills men, it is worry. Work is healthy; you can hardly put more on a man than he can bear. But worry is rust upon the blade. It is not movement that destroys the machinery, but friction. Never let life's hardships disturb us no one can avoid problems, not even saints or sages. As with any habit, the habit of remaining positive in all situations takes practice and a commitment to us to take control. Life is what you make it, so make it a happy one!! Don't worry on things that may not happen, life is too short to worry too much. Smile and be happy.

CHAPTER TWELVE

FEW STEPS TO LEAD A TENSION FREE AND HAPPY LIFE

It is often said that mindfulness meditation helps people to develop the skill of being detached and aware. As a result we can become aware of these core irrational beliefs about self, others, and the world without activating self-destructive survival behaviors driven by high stress. We ought to know the simple ways to get people into using mindfulness meditation.. A little stress to keep us energized motivated and hanging out with the people that are doing healthy things. Having a stable relationship these all the primarily things we ought to gather within ourselves.

We have to be on the lookout for a possible date with someone. We may even join special groups or clubs of people within our age bracket and who share the same interest. Join church events as well. Try new activities. By expanding our horizon, we will get to know more people who can be a potential date of having a good company.

Let us keep life simple. Many of us are always over looking for the most complicated way of doing things in life. We can make our lives to be more simple just take a walk through the park, or a quiet evening with the family. We need not clutter our lives with unnecessary decisions by making everything complicated and complex why not try to keep it simple.

Why not practice to be satisfied.

Many people don't know how to be satisfied with what life gives them. They are so busy wanting more that they squander what life has already given them. Always urging for more and demanding to have everything making themselves and lives more complicated. Why not practice to be more satisfied we need most.

What we need to beware is of indecision.

Life is not that easy at times we have to make tough choices. Never put off a decision that we can make on the day. At times we may miss some of the best and most exciting opportunities in the world because we were indecisive. People who are successful people do not fall prey back and forth on decisions.

Let us practice cheerfulness and be happy

We have heard it several times before, and we would hear it here again and again – it only takes a few seconds to smile! We need not be surprised as to how well being cheerful to others can spread like wildfire and make us happy. We live in a society where often glumness is the ruled. A simple smile or kind word can spread through our culture like a fire – not only will we feel better, but those who interact with us will also feel better and best. Therefore why we should not practice cheerfulness and make ourselves happy.

How about if we learn to like people and make ourselves happy. We don't have to love everyone we meet; we simply need to learn to like people – especially those who are different than us. Often we may not agree with everything what they do, or maybe with all of their beliefs, but by learning to get along with them we will open our mind up to change – a critical trait that is absolutely necessary in world of today. The most important thing that we must learn is to Live and let live. Is it really our concern what the guy across the other lane wants to do something with his life or wants to share his life with? Why not we learn to live our lives to the fullest and let others live their life to their fullest. We need to bear in mind that we are not above anyone else, and none of us should think we should be allowed to dictate how another person should live and lead their lives.

Stop beating over the past happening and let us forgive ourselves. It is simple let us stop beating things that happened in the past – things what we have done or we did not do, and the awful mistakes that we may have made. Forgiving oneself is a unique skill and only few of us have the ability to accomplish. It's such a shame that we spent a lifetime living in the past and never make it to our full potential in the future. We must forgive ourselves – and just as importantly, forgive others too. It may seem to be a difficult task but if we encourage each other and stop beating over the past we will live a more meaningful, happy and fulfilled life...........

CHAPTER THIRTEEN

SIGNIFICANCE OF DIFFERENT SIGNS ZODIAC SIGNS

ARIES (21st March –19th April)

Your Ruling Planet   Mars
Your Sign   Fiery
Born in Sign   Movable

CHARACTERISTIC

Your shall have round eyes, shall be quite talkative and urguementive. Short tempered, angry and bilious in nature. Tend to be the eldest of of the children, shall be popular, stingy and unsteady in behavior, moment of arms, hands and fingers are frequently seen while in conversation with others. Full of vigor, honored by the government, sparingly eating habits and shall have few children in life.
Appearance:

A good physique with large bones. Your features and your teeth tend to be good and even you are of medium height and you tend to develop into a unique punchy personality.

Personality:

You possess forceful, courageous, enterprising and industrious instincts. You refuse to give up until and unless you have not achieved your targets.

Winning or losing is not very important to you, giving a good effort and showing a good account of your abilities is quite something where you are more cautious about. In your approach and speech you are quite confident even though you are not equipped with much knowledge of that subject.

You are straightforward in your speech and would often not; hesitate in calling a thief a thief.

Calling a thief a thief doesn't always make you popular and even though you're fully aware of this, you really wont care much about others feeling and shall stick to your comments. You neither like pressures being forced upon you nor would like subordination, but would rather wish to be free in thoughts and action, and would love, free style of functioning. You are best suited for guiding, controlling and governing others. You can be very self-assertive, and well equipped to deal with any situation or emergency when the situation demands. You tend to be over optimistic and too impulsive and later regret your actions or inaction and at times overshoot the mark or over trade in business. Because of your impulsiveness you don't hesitate to get into an argument or pick up a quarrel over petty things. You are not the kind of person who would look before you leap, consistency is also not your virtue. Even if you happen to occupy a humble or subordinate position you will try to be at the head of some branch of your work or assignment. Whether in profession or business you will cross all barriers and speed breakers to attain success.

Profession and Career

You are best suited for a career connected with Metals, Engineering, Metallurgy, Surgery and you often tend to become good trade union leaders. Explorers, Explosives, Teachers, Self-Employed Professionals or the business people. Dealers of firearms, Dentists, Mechanics, and Sportsmen are the other fields where you would excel well.

Business and Finances

Though you have a good head for business but when it comes to making investments or tying up new deals, your become quite impulsive and rash. With the result your profits are cut off or minimized, but your financial position remain quite stable.

As you're prone to overrating your own judgment, it is you're over confidence, which combines with your impulsiveness that cuts off or reduces your profits. However, you're able to pull back yourself from major disasters and you do not remain a debtor for long.

You Match with Aries, Leo Scorpions and Sagittarius

Romance and Marriage

You warm hearted nature will provide you with excellent chance for love and romance. But you must restrain yourself from being rash and impulsive. You expect your loved ones to share your thoughts and to respond to your moods in all situations. Your love life is quite stylish, and your living is luxurious. Romance and Love means a lot to you and you not hesitate in keeping every thing aside until you get your desires fulfilled.

YOUR WEAKNESS

You will be such a bad liar that others can immediately see through you. But however selfish you may be, you will feel the sense of your selfishness if pointed out to you and you will readily accept the fact. Since you are a quick-witted, restless character, you may find it too difficult to be patient in any situation, which you do not like. You will put up with adverse conditions only as long as you are confident about it and you will eventually bring about the changes as per your desire and wishes even though you may have to take unnecessary risks in achieving your goals. Bravery and disregard for danger are inheritance in you.

You have the capacity to rapidly grasp the essential of a situation, but you shall also have its drawbacks, for not in seeing the whole shape of a problem, they might appear to be resulting in an argument, and leading to give an offence. You may be quick-tempered, but will be at your worst, extremely selfish, and demanding if such an occasion arises.

Health and Disease

The body parts ruled by your sign are muscles, head, and the eyes, and the face. You are quite prone to headaches, head injuries, brain disorders, and burns, are the other positive pointers. Minor accidents are also not ruled out.

You are person who could be recognized by a fine facial bone structure with a shining healthy head of hair. Definitely you are not weak people. You are mostly in a hurry and often do not get time to eat properly, with the result you tend to suffer from stomach ailments because low diet. At times you are subject to blood pressure, heart-related problems, and headaches including sinus and migraines.

As most conditions apply, plenty of water is essential for your body and you should take regular diet and complete rest, whenever excess stress or strain is promulgated.

Lucky Day   Tuesday
Lucky Colors   Red and white.
Lucky Stones   Red Coral, Ruby, Garnet Blood Stone.
Lucky Numbers 9, 18, 27, 36, 45, 54, 63 and 7

TAURUS (20th April -20th May)

Your Ruling Planet	Venus
Your Sign	Earth
Born in Sign	Fixed

CHARACTERISTIC

Ruled by Venus, the planet of love, you are good and sympathetic, caring and loyal. It is often said that you are a good lover of beauty. Your sense of preservation is far developed. Your strong will power generally carries you to great heights even when you are under severe stress and strain conditions. You have tendency to put on weight even though you are strong and well built. You love to have good food and prefer to take high fat diet and enjoy living in comfortable surroundings. At times when you tend to be lazy, and unwilling to do the job or work assigned to you, with the result that you loss the fruitful gains that are stored for you.

You're concerned with gaining material wealth and status and you make a sincere effort in achieving them. You have excellent business sense, the ability to make money. You are generous in entertaining your friends, and you enjoy the company of friends much more than the others do. You shall feel happier living in the big cities rather than in small towns.

Appearance

You are well built and hefty and you tend to put on weight easily. Your eyes are attractive and your body appearance resembles to a bull. Your lips are well shaped and your skin is soft and glowing. Your movements are quite graceful and well matched. You have broad face stout shoulders with big belly.

Personality

You are a popular learned and sensuous personality. You are practical, persevering and you have good powers of endurance. You often make faithful and loyal friends. You are very careful about your personal comforts and money matters. You are unreasonably stubborn at times, and you lose other people' sympathy in process. You have great power of endurance and patience, but when provoked to anger, your become wild, volatile and would not mind using abusive language. You have a strong will power and are quite conservative in your thoughts and actions.

You are bit slow but steady in actions. You would not to waste surplus energy and talent. You would plodder around a subject for pretty long till you are sure about it. You would only than act fast and wisely and see to it, that the concerned matters go to your advantage and favor. You are fond of ease, comforts and luxuries. You become worldly and take pleasure in the good things of life.

Profession and Careers

You would have a good taste for Arts, Music, Theatre, and Cinema. You would also make good singers, dancers, and art and jewelry dealers. Writers, models, actors are the other fields where you excel pretty well. Architects, financiers, bankers, are optional field, which fancy you.

Business and Finances

You make excellent business people and financiers and are known as the money zone of the zodiac. You manage to find opportunities to increase your profits or expand your business where others see none. You also tend to instinctively find above average avenues of investment. The best deals that you strike are generally those connected with land or property. You work happily as Florist, in Livestock or Poultry industry or are often seen as heads of Super Markets and wholesale food industrialist.

You Match with

Taurus, Gemini Virgo, Capricorn, and Aquarius.

Romance and Marriage

Since Venus, which powers you with physical charm, governs you happen to become a good humorist, thus radiating warmth and vitality around you. You are amorous by nature and you find it difficult to restrain the affections one bestowed upon you. You are also easily influenced by the attraction of the opposite sex. You make friends easily and are quite popular with fairer sex. Its a different matter that your romance begins only after you have satisfied yourself or have observed that your partner has the qualities that appeal to you. You are emotionally attached to their spouse once married, you look for unshakable stability. Your patience in personal relationships ensures you with stability and smoothness. You generally full fill your duties and obligations towards your loved ones.

Health and Disease

Though you are a good eater of delicious foods you would at the same time. Love to exercise and help your self in maintaining good health. Your sign rules, tongue and ears, the neck, throat, vocal chords, tonsils, thyroid gland, chin, lower jaw. You are prone to colds, coughs, sore throats, tonsillitis, obesity, blood pressure and constipation.

YOUR WEAKNESS

You can easily be misled by emotions and affections. You tend to be quite jealous and sentimental with regards to the matter of sex. You are dominating and obstinate with the result you almost lose the ground, which you have gained during your interaction with opposite sex. But once you find that everything around you is smooth and the grass is green and lovely you plunge head long to build a happy home and would like to create a world of your own nature.

Lucky Day   Friday
Lucky Colors   Blue and violet
Lucky Stones   Diamond, white zircon.
Lucky Numbers 6, 15, 24, 33, 42 and 51

GEMINI (21st May to 20th June)

Your Ruling Planet	MERCURY
Your Sign	AIR
Born in Sign	Movable

CHARACTERISTIC

You are an airy sign you live mostly in the mind. You will be carefree, joyous and reluctant. Your mind will be strong and positive and strong. You are often versatile. Restless and inclined to changes and make improvements whenever there is necessity. You also appreciate traveling in search of adventure and amusement. Your enjoyment of the use of words enhances your ability to converse. You are quick, perceptive, clever, playful and imaginative, and you express yourself to feel alive. You feel fresh when you can move around mentally and physically unrestricted. Your ability to bluff your way out of tight corners is phenomenal, and you will always be on the go. You will be doing more than one thing at a time. This dual phenomenon is an important part of your nature. You need plenty of variety and change. You can very easily become bored, and your answer to drop whatever is boring to you is quite certain and to take, the next job in hand is one of your charactericts. You should be careful not to overstrain your sensitive nervous system, which can break down under pressure. You enjoy mental recreation, but you also appreciate traveling in search of adventure and amusement.

If you're not interested in something, you can be indifferent to your liking and friendship. You love to be in company and attempt a whole variety of things simultaneously.

Appearance

Describing the Gemini is as mercurial is right on the money, since Gemini is ruled by the Planet Mercury. Moving, restless, seeking, learning -- Gemini is constant motion, a torrent of wind which is in keeping with this sign's element of Air. The Twins are highly intellectual and won't hesitate to play mind games with a lover, mere child's play to them. They are also great communicators, so get ready to hear everything from pithy remarks to impassioned pleas. Inventive, quick-witted and fun, the Twins will jump around from one lover to the next until they find one which is almost as smart as they are and able to keep up in this high-spirited race. The reward for those who can lasso a Gemini is a free-spirited lover who shines at parties but is also a devil in the bedroom.

Personality

A fine bone structure and movements that are light often set you apart from others and make you good dancers as well. Your facial expressions are usually baby like in their transparency. Quick to smile, with ears that are a bit larger than normal, your physique tends to remain slim even when your food intake begins to cross the limits. The Gemini is always right and never changes his mind - until the next time the argument comes around, when he will take a totally different stand, and deny ever having given vent to his earlier opinions. This is infuriating for his opponents in argument, especially as he has a considerable talent for dialogue - and a tendency to know a very little about a very great number of things, and to master this knowledge skillfully as to seem well informed. His ability to bluff his way out of tight corners is phenomenal. There then, are his worst faults - inconsistency and superficiality.

Little wonder, perhaps, that the world's most popular journalists in newspaper, radio, and television are Gemini's. For again, they have an insistent urge to communicate.

Profession and Career

You would make good writers, radio and TV producers or anchor people, lecturers, linguists, teachers, travel agents, sales people.

Business and Finances

Like air, you feel fresh when you can move around mentally and physically unrestricted. But when traveling, you're likely to take along beepers, mobile phones, laptop computers, portable radios and televisions, and remote controls. You like being busy, juggling two or more things at once. Boredom, censure or repression could make you impatient, restless, anxious, snappish, sarcastic, gossipy, cynical or nervously exhausted

You Match with Leo Gemini, Libra and Aquarius

Romance and Marriage

A love affair with a Gemini requires great stamina; so start doing those push-ups now! The Twins are both fun and funny and love to laugh, play and romp. They are possessed of a very active mind, which can sometimes lead to a short attention span. The best way to keep the Twins around, and aroused, is through mental stimulation. A razor-sharp and imaginative lover is a godsend to the terrific Twins. This sign also values adventure and travel, so a certain footloose and fancy free-ness will help this romance bloom.

The duality of the Twins allows them to see both sides of an issue, so in times of stress, they are much likelier to be a lover than a fighter. They will also feel especially connected to those who can help them feel, since they spend so much of their time thinking. It's true that your attentions tend to stray even after marriage but it's also true that responsibilities gradually change your attitude and force you into being steady wives and husbands. And yet, you love your home and family and want the best for them. Resolving contradictions where you want to remain free and yet have a good family life are essential for you.

YOUR WEAKNESS

Someone who can roll with the punches and keep smiling in the face of a multi-faceted onslaught is priceless to the hyperactive Twins. It's an added plus if that person is smart, fun, a good friend and a great sport. Gemini's need someone who can be attentive to them and who will naturally enjoy their sparkle and wit. They also prefer a strong partner who is not necessarily as smart as they are but who can pick them up, emotionally, when necessary. If the Twins can make a marvelous mental match, life will be a dream. The Gemini lover is easygoing and caring, yet daring and a ball of fire at the right moments. Mental fireworks are high on their agenda, their own as well as those they can make with another. Only those with plenty of punch need apply for this celestial light show! The Gemini is always right and never changes his mind - until the next time the argument comes around, when he will take a totally different stand, and deny ever having given vent to his earlier opinions. This is infuriating for his opponents in argument, especially as he has a considerable talent for dialogue - and a tendency to know a very little about a very great number of things, and to master this knowledge skillfully as to seem well informed. His ability to bluff his way out of tight corners is phenomenal. There, then, are his worst faults - inconsistency and superficiality. Little wonder, perhaps, that the world's most popular journalists in newspaper, radio, and television are Gemini's. For again, they have an insistent urge to communicate.

Health and Disease

You suffer from allergies, asthma and frequent colds and flu. The skin, hair, veins as well as throat, kidneys and lumbar region of Gemini's get easily affected.

Lucky Day   Wednesday
Lucky Color   Yellow
Lucky Stones   Yellow Carnelian Agate)
Lucky Numbers   3, 12, 21, 30, 48, 57

CANCER (22nd June-22nd July)

Your Ruling Planet   Moon
Your sign   Water
Born in Sign   Movable

CHARACTERISTIC

You are changeable, moody, restless and sensitive. You are emotional, tenacious, honest, intelligent, industrious, and miserly. Though proud, talkative, quite independent in your feelings, you are more attached to your home and family.

Physical Appearance

Usually of medium height, your build is sturdy and stocky. Your complexion is generally smooth and free from pimples and blemishes. Most of you have a strong, muscular physique with largish bones. Even symmetrical teeth and a wide mouth.

Personality

Your sign of water makes your nature moody. You tend to keep your emotions hidden in the innermost of your heart. This watery sign also bestows the powers of intuition. You possess strong pioneering instincts and are generally enterprising and industrious. In crunch situations, you are forceful a courageous and refuse to give up until you have achieved your targets or at least put in your best. Like a true sportsperson, you like to play for the challenge and enjoyment and at one level, winning or losing is not so important, what matters more to you is giving a good account of yourself. You are sensitive and take a fancy to any thing, which comes new to you. In your speech and approach, you are direct and forthright. You are very particular about having good food. You're generally easy to get along with.

Your bad eating habits may often lead you to bad health. You don't like pressures being on you and value an easy going, free style of functioning. You tend to be too impulsive and later regret your actions or inaction. You're often also too outspoken and undiplomatic.

Profession and Career

Being hard working and industrious, you are successful in your own profession and business. You often reach high position in life. You generally make good Engineers, Explorers, Metal Workers, Dentists, Surgeons, Mechanics, Self-employed Professionals or Business People. You do well in teaching, writing, painting, advertising, and selling things and also in trade and commerce, particularly, imports and exports.

Business and Finance

Although you have a good head for business and your financial position is usually stable, you're prone to overrating your own judgment, especially when it comes to making investments or tying up new deals. It's your impulsive nature and you're over confidence, which combine to cut it to your profits. Generally, however, you're able to pull back from major disasters and the saving grace is that you'll never remain a debtor. You are highly ambitious when it comes to amassing wealth, but you have to climb an uphill task in achieving the same. Wealth often eludes you even when you inherit your parental property or wealth. You should avoid betting, speculation and horseracing, as you are more likely to lose, rather than gain.

You Match with

Cancer, Leo, Scorpio, Sagittarius and Pisces

Romance and Marriage

You will enjoy your family life. Home and family are of great importance to you and will manage to keep your spouse quite happy and gay. You have a good style of admiration and you indulge in light flirtations. Many of you, despite your deep-seated desire to set up a home, are averse to marriage.

Part of the reason for this is that you are unable to disclose your inmost emotions and feelings even when your heart beats in tune to a strong love tone. Often, you tend to be attracted to an opposite number. Love means a lot to you and you're generally willing to put everything else aside until it fulfills your desires. Warm and loving, you often shower your through various means which includes paying profuse compliments, showering gifts, making stylish dates. Whether you're a male or a female you are usually very frank and forthright and you like to make it clear at the outset itself whether you're simply flirting or whether you are serious in your love and romantic affairs.

HEALTH AND DISEASE

You are likely to suffer from water born diseases, comprising of gastric trouble, inflammatory troubles of liver, minor boils and infection in stomach. At times mental depression and excitement. Diabetes is one factor, where you need to be beware of.

YOUR WEAKNESS

You are lustful, drunkard and fickle minded. You become irritable and your crooked eyes speak of your lust and greed at several occasions.

Lucky Colors   Green, mauve, mountain blue.
Lucky Stones   Emerald, pearl, cat's eye.
Your Lucky Numbers 2, 11, 20 29,

LEO (23rd July-22nd August)

Your Planetary Ruler   Sun
Your Element   Fire
Born in Sign   Fixed

CHARACTERISTIC

You are extremely sympathetic, generous, honest, straightforward and authoritative. You are honest, frank, and outspoken. You are enterprising and like to command. In fact, your strongest instinct is to rule and command. You love authority. You are quite proud and lucky in money matters. You possess a strong will power and you achieve your objectives in spite of the difficulties or obstacles that come in your way. You are enterprising, soft but outspoken helpful and righteous personality. You are sincere, reputed, independent, impatient bold, generous and a respectable person. A traveler, obstinate and a happy go lucky person. You are affectionate, enthusiastic, cheerful, and optimistic whom, bring sunshine into other lives.

Appearance

You are tall, physically strong, and attractive and have a fair complexion. You have broad shoulders and have beautiful eyes with abundant energy. Your constitution is generally robust; you appear to have fashioned round face with model looks.

Personality

You are inclined to quick anger. Success comes to you only after much struggle. You would remain devoted to your parents. Your wife would be virtuous and happy lady.

Physically, you are strong and if you happen to fall ill, you will recover soon. You are both courageous and valorous. You never want to giveaway. You shun inferior jobs and are fond of a life of luxury works and jobs. You have a strong desire to travel, and you prefer to have an aristocratic society.

Professions and Career

The career best suited for you are Civil Services, Finance, Politics, Armed Forces, Business of Commanding Nature, You are quite courteous, diplomatic and do well in all professions where you may have to deal with dignified people. You are not generally good in dealing with masses or where laborers are involved. Your life starts to boom and you have the tendency to earn money at much younger age.

Business and Finances

You are magnanimous and are, therefore, unable to save in proportion to your income. Business partnerships lead to litigation, which should be settled out of court. There is a danger of part of your property being destroyed by fire. In financial matters, you may not get a square deal from your brothers and sisters, and this may even lead to litigation.

You Match With Aries, Leo, Sagittarius and Gemini.

Romance and Marriage

You love steadfastly, and usually get married fairly early. However, being stubborn, you do not have a smooth relationship with your partner. You want to be overbearing, and unless the partner is submissive and docile, this leads to frequent clashes.

YOUR WEAKNESS

You tend to have a lot of ego and pride, and you have a certain amount of vanity by which you are easily ruffled. Your inimical feelings continue for a long time. You are pompous and prefer to show off your splendor on many occasions. You at times get suspicious, even when there is no substantial cause. You are inclined towards betting, gambling speculation, and games of chance. The greed of becoming rich at one go often attracts you.

HEALTH AND DISEASE

The heart and the aorta, upper back, spleen and the spinal chord form your major vulnerable health areas and can result in heart diseases, back problems, or spinal meningitis. Your sign rules the heart and back, and your tendency to drive yourself hard, often puts them under pressure. The pressure increases because you enjoy good food and are prone to be overweight. For good health, you've got to respect your body's needs.

Lucky Days	Sundays
Lucky Color	Red, orange, gold white.
Lucky Stones	Ruby, amber, diamonds.
Your Lucky Numbers	1, 10, 28, 37, 46, 55

VIRGO (23rd August to 22nd September)

Your Planetary Ruler	Mercury
Your Element	Earth
Your Sign	Movable

Characteristics

You are attractive, modest, reserved, honest, long armed, with drooping shoulders, sweet speech, intelligent, fond of pleasure, music and opposite sex.

Physical Appearance

Often of a small build, you have a large fund bustling energy and are seldom able to sit still for long. Your noses a seldom bulbous, and your lips are generally delicately shaped. Your sky tends to be soft and oily in your younger years.

Personality

You are discriminating, analytical, objective and practical. As a result, you excel in all work in which analysis and critical judgment is required. You have great clarity in your thoughts and strong powers of discerning hidden things. However, although you have a strong love for justice, you are only moderately sympathetic towards others. You are cool-headed and balanced. Happily, you are not vindictive and in fact, quite shy, prefer to work quietly and in seclusion. You are likely to travel a great deal for business or pleasure.

Travel brings good luck and addition to fortune.

By and large, you will rise by dint of your personal efforts and merit. Once aroused, it's difficult for you to cool down. You also tend to live in your imagination far too often.

Profession and Career

You would do well in all occupations connected with higher sciences, mechanics, dietetics, nutrients, health, and labour. Since you go into details, you are industrious, and are devoted to your work. You make good executives, organizers and directors. You are an earthy sign, and if you have an inclination for agriculture and horticulture, you can successful in any occupation connected with land.

Business and Finances

Acquisition of wealth will prove an uphill task. Though the struggle will be hard and beset with many difficulties, you will triumph ultimately due to intelligent handling and hard work. You will, however, have secret enemies, and should be very careful in your investments.

Ideal Match

Taurus, Virgo and Capricorn.

Romance and Marriage

Your love life is not smooth as a rule, partly because you have high expectations always. There are, chances of second marriage. Even if there is no second marriage, there may be a long-standing attachment. Many of you have a tendency to fall in love at a comparatively young age, but such a relationship is seldom enduring.

Health and Disease

Your health is, generally, not good in childhood, but as the years pass, and it becomes better. You are likely to have complaints of the bowels and weakness of the sympathetic nervous system, the abdomen and the liver, the gall bladder and gall ducts. Virgos are very fussy food eaters. You are anemic and suffer from indigestion, gas pains, ulcers, liver upsets, colitis and bowel problems

Lucky Days   Wednesday, Saturday.
Lucky Colors   Orange, Yellow, Grey, White.
Lucky Stones   Emerald, Jade, amethyst, topaz.
Your Lucky Numbers 5, 14, 50, 59 68 and 77

LIBRA (23rd September to 22nd October)

Your ruling planet	Venus
Your Element	Air
Your sign	Movable

CHARACTERISTIC

Libra being the seventh sign of the zodiac and is ruled by the Planet Venus. You are attractive, tall and have a very sharp nose. You are intelligent, learned, religious, lover of beautiful things of nature and fond of pleasures. AS you possess sound judgments you are clever at making schemes. You are quite popular, lover of Art and Music.

Physical Appearance

Physically, you don't appear to be too strong and robust at first glance but you actually have great stamina. Your skin usually has a healthy glow to it and people often envy the texture of your hair.

Personality

You are gentle, compassionate and have an affectionate nature. You are large-hearted, with strong passions. You have a keen sense of honor and justice. In case of a dispute, friends and acquaintances are likely to turn to you as an arbitrator.

If you are appointed as judges, you keep the scales even. You have a keen aesthetic sense as well, and are fond of beauty and symmetry. Your judgments are on the dot but sometimes, you tend to be hesitant and indecisive, preferring to err on the side of diplomacy and tact. You often achieve a good position in life due to unexpected assistance from relatives. In religious matters, you are broad-minded, and want to follow the good and moral tenets of all religions and philosophies. However, you meet serious opposition in life from people in the field of religion and law.

Profession

You succeed in law, art, music, dealing in merchandise, mechanics, or professions connected with wines, spirits and liquors, science and navigation. Advocates, you make good Actors, Judges, Politicians, Diplomats and Salespersons.

Business and Finances

You seldom find yourself in a position where you have to take a loan. You often come into riches through a marriage or by entering into a business partnership. You build up your finances step-by-step for the future, and purchase property by paying regular installments.

You Match with Gemini, Libra or Aquarius.
Romance and Marriage

You are inclined to go through more than one relationship before deciding whom to marry. You are affectionate by nature, and make good friends. Sometimes your friendship is mistaken as love by the opposite sex. You should in fact avoid self-indulgence in matters of sex and affection, and should not enter into bonds of matrimony with the first person you like

Your weakness

You often spend your energy taking care of others instead of yourself. Plenty of water is necessary in a day for you as this keeps you away from toxins. Proper rest is very necessary for your health. So it would be advisable on your part to take proper rest and not to over exhort yourself.

Health and Disease

You are likely to suffer from diseases of the bowels, the bladder, the kidneys, the lumbar region, and the spine. At times, however, you tend to be a bit of a hypochondriac, worrying about your health and that of family members, even when no serious ailments are anywhere on the horizon. You are pretty healthy people but still you are prone to weakness in the lower back when you over exert yourself. You suffer from allergies, asthma and frequent colds and flu. The skin, hair, veins as well as throat, kidneys and lumbar region of you get easily affected.

Lucky Days   Fridays, Mondays.
Lucky Colors   Blue, green and white.
Lucky Stones   Sapphire, Turquoise Opal.
Your Lucky Numbers 6, 15, 42, 51, 60

SCORPIO (24th October to 21st November)

Your Planetary Ruler   Mars Pluto
Your Element   Water
Your sign   Fixed

Characterizes

You have a well-set body and are of middle structure, you have a youthful appearance and are fickle minded fellow. You are clever powerful and dignified at the same time you are cruel, sensual and usually not generous. You are a good conversationalist and you possess equally good writing skills, and are of commanding nature.

Physical Appearance

Generally, you present an attractive and strikingly tidy appearance with not a hair out of place, your nails well cared for and so on. Most of you have a fine skin texture. However, once you have entered your thirties, you tend to put on weights.

Personality

You have a strong and dominating personality, with strong will power. Generally, you never forget a grudge, and take revenge even after a long time. You do not prefer a frontal attack, and opt for indirect means. Subtle strategies and conspiracies hold a special fascination for you.

Therefore, you must be specially beware of who may happen to be your enemies. You are not only subtle, but energetic too. Generally, people around you are quick to note that you have a keen and penetrating Intellect, combined with great dynamism. You are also analytical, skilful and patient, and have literary abilities and creative talents.

Profession and Career

The most suitable professions for you are those related to music, art and scientific pursuits. You also do well as doctors, particularly, as surgeons in departments of public health. You make good Architects, Executives in Industry, Officers in the Military and Navy, Chemists, Heads of Institutions, Mechanical engineers, Machinists, Sales Managers.

Business and Finances

You are shrewd at business matters, and financially, you generally do well. But you like to make a lot of money all at once. You have to be patient and persevering in building your finances. You should adopt wait and watch policy rather than grabbing all the entire lot at one time.

Ideal Match Cancer, Scorpio and Pisces.
Romance and Marriage

Love and Romance are the basic instincts of your harmful life. You are prone to get attraction of the opposite sex. In spite of your refusal to accept the pure love of the opposite sex you easily get on facial attraction rather than true love. You are considered very sexy and are intense lovers, with the attraction being more of physical craving than pure love. In several cases it has been noticed that probably there may be a tragedy in the first part of your life, and you may marry a second time.

Health and Disease

Your health calls for more care and attention. Since you are a good eater of delicious food you should be more careful in your choice of food. You are also prone to fevers and bruises. The weak parts in your anatomy are the groin and bladder, the pelvis, the stomach and the throat. You are prone to catching infections and contagious diseases.

Your Weakness

You generally put off things till the last moment and you also prepare at the eleventh hour it is because of your fortune that you come out successfully. You have the tendency to start late but again your fortune favors you to finish first. Though on the face it you appear to be frank playful and blunt but actually you would like to keep all secrets in your heart and mind.

Lucky Days   Tuesday and Thursday.
Lucky Colors   Rust, red, earth brown.
Lucky Stone   Bloodstone, Topaz, Garnet, Red Coral.
Your Lucky Numbers 9, 18, 36, 45,

SAGITTARIUS (22nd November to 21st December)

Your Planetary Ruler   Jupiter
Your Element   Fire
Your sign   Movable

Character tics

You are well known for your boldness and dashing approach in relationship and conversations. You are courageous pushy and accommodating. You being a dual sign you believe in that variety is this spice of life. You also insist on your personal freedom and liberty.

Appearance

Generally fine boned with a glowing complexion, large eyes, a pert nose and a charming smile, you tend to walk with a gliding movement. Your bodily actions are usually soft and refined instead of being clumsy and ungainly.

Personality

You are usually quite brilliant, noble and refined. You are swift and sudden in speech and action. Sometimes you speak out your mind even before the other person has finished a sentence. You are truthful, and keep your promises. You are bold, free and dashing. You make friends easily, and are attached to them.

You are socially successful, and many persons of high standing will become your patrons. But some of them will prove to be highly treacherous, and will almost result in your loss of position. Your enemies will prove to be very bitter and persistent. You should take care that your position and prosperity are not threatened by the mischief of your enemies. You have a strong instinct, and are more successful if you work according to your own instincts, rather than on the advice of others. You should avoid betting, speculation and gambling, as this habit may lead to heavy losses.

Profession and Career

You can succeed well in teaching, in the field of religion and law, in politics, administration, and also in business or banking. You are good sports persons, fond of hunting and the outdoor life and would do well in any occupation connected with them. You have a strong dramatic sense as well, and can also do well in occupations connected with the stage.

Business and Finances

Your early years will not be prosperous. You may be subjected to financial stringency on account of losses your parents may have suffered. Success will come to you only after middle age. Up to your thirtieth year, you are likely to have frequent setbacks in your financial career. But success does come to you, as your sun sign is ruled by Jupiter, which stands for honor, riches and position. You do not have a strong inclination towards purchase of real estate and immovable properties. Consequently, very few persons born under this sun sign build large estates.

Ideal Match Aries, Leo, Sagittarius and Pisces.

Romance and Marriage

In choosing your spouse, you are more idealistic than passionate. Consequently, even after the engagement, you break off the relationship if you find that your finance is not up to your mark. You love, but since you are not demonstrative in your affections, others may misunderstand them as lacking in warmth. However, if your spouse fails to keep in pace with you, the marriage may break. At times, there are two marriages, one of which proves detrimental to your progress.

Health and Disease

Your general health is good, but you are likely to suffer from nervous disorders. The sign Sagittarius rules the hips, thighs and the muscular system. It is also connected with the motor impulses. You are likely to suffer from mental tension, Sciatica, Hip Disease or some kind of lameness.

YOUR WEAKNESS

You being a masculine sing, you do not hesitate to think and you speak out and act, as you desire. Though you are truthful in your thoughts people will misunderstand and take you as their enemies because of your harsh and bold talks, you will speak out what you feel is right without considering how the others would value your such statements. You are advice not to be out spoken if you want to maintain your relationship with others.

Lucky Days   Monday and Thursday
Lucky Colors   Red, Pink, and Purple.
Lucky Stones   Topaz, and Turquoise.
Your Lucky Numbers 3, 12, 21, 39, 48

CAPRICORN (22nd December to 19th January)

Your Planetary Ruler   Saturn
Your Element   Earth
Your sign   Moveable

Characteristics

You will be economical, prudent, reasonable, thoughtful and practical in life. You will be calculative and you will execute any work after taking a thoughtful and careful decision. You will have the required push and confidence and you will not hesitate in bringing through chance in your career, once you take a bold and careful decision you have a study nature, immense tolerance but at times you will lack the required degree of patience. You are serious in disposition, and humility is one of your chief characteristics.

Appearance

You are good looking, with sharp features, well shaped eyebrows and sensual lips. Your eyes are piecing in their intensity at times. You facial outlook is also quite pleasing and attraction.

Personality

You are prudent, cautious and hard working. You are active and vigorous, and, at the same time, plodding. You are endowed with a spirit of service, and have a strong sense of duty. You have initiative that brings you success. You are practical and economical in spending. You are loyal and conscientious in your work. Your practical nature, at times, gives the impression that you lack warmth. But actually, you are loving and devoted. You will meet opposition from persons occupying high or low ranks, but will, ultimately, surmount all obstacles. You will have powerful patronage of a very high personage, particularly, if you are in the armed forces. In service, you will give satisfaction to your superior. You often rise high in politics too.

Profession and Career

You succeed well in all occupations where hard work and plodding are the main features. You do well in work connected with Agriculture, Forestry, Education, Biology, in Factories and large organizations.

Business and Finances

You are versatile and shrewd in business. You earn money on your own and not due to any windfall, legacy or inheritance. Money also comes to you late in life. You have to toil pretty hard to get to the highest position in life. Money does not come to you that easily.

Ideal Match Taurus, Virgo, Libra and Capricorn.

Romance and Marriage

You do not marry in a hurry, and do so only when you are assured that the other party reciprocates your love. However, you do not prove stable in your affections.

This is not due to an inborn unfaithful disposition but due to the influence of others. Your spouse may be fickle, and bring about a break in your marital relationship. Often, you prefer to marry a homebody who can provide home comforts and good companionship.

Health and Disease

You are likely to suffer from rheumatism or gout. You are liable to get liver trouble nervous tension should be avoided. Your stomach is weak spot. Your health gets better with your age. You tend to suffer from joint problems, arthritis, neuralgia and rheumatism. You are prone to skin diseases and have problems with bones, gall bladder, teeth and spleen.

Your Weakness

You often tend to become desperate, broken hearted and test yourself to a greater height where you feel the burden of physical strain. Therefore you should correct yourselves and you should be aware of others as well as your fault and deficiency you should avoid nervousness at all cost.

Lucky Days   Saturday
Lucky Colors   Grey, black, blue, brown.
Lucky Stones   Blue Sapphire, Amethyst, Onyx.
Lucky Numbers 1, 10, 4, 22, 35, 44

AQUARIUS (20th January to 18th February)

Your Ruling Planet   Saturn, Uranus
Your Element   Air
Born in Sign: Fixed

CHARACTERISTIC

Being the eleventh sign of the zodiac, you have a broad outlook and human understanding. You are outspoken, social, intelligent, and you possess good retentive power. You are also shrewd, clever headed you have your own way of thinking and doing things and you carry out your works according to your own discretion. You will not hesitate to do any unusual or irregular thing even if you consider tobe morally upright. Your sense of dressing and the taste of clothing would be something different and you not like to imitate others. You have your individuality, mannerism peculiarity and your own specialty. You are often far ahead with fresh ideas and schemes. You generate new ideas and at times act in a way which shows that the laws are not made for you which means you over act and your actions are beyond anything body's imagination. You develop good intuition and mental will prefer to go for deep meditation and good concentration.

Appearance

You are middle stature strong person and have broad shoulder and large bones with a little amount of grace and your physical appearance is quite striking. Quite of you possess high cheeks and a peculiar winning smile.

Personality

You have an alert mind, and are keen to acquire more knowledge. You have striking intuitive and psychic powers. You possess a strong will power, and are hard working. You are fond of solitude, and are patient and persevering in your efforts. You are religious and philosophical. You see religion and philosophy as a manifestation of beauty and harmony, a means of universal love and service to mankind. You have a logical mind, and would do well to be guided by your own intuition and reasoning rather than that of others in arriving at decisions. You are kind hearted, original, simple, energetic and systematic. You are honest to your friends and enjoy enormous respect in your group.

Your friends and contacts will range from many influential and eminent people yet you will feel melancholy and lonely at times. You will be ready to help others at the moment's notice but will always remain personally detached. You are an idealist independent, inventive thinker, quick witted, positive, excitable and, when need be you are also aggressive and combative.

Profession and Career

Since you a scientific bent of mind the profession and career best suited for you are Finance Marketing, Administration, Writing, Physiologists, Acting and you excel well when you are given the chance to handle most difficult situation or posts. You are also excellent when it comes to public dealing and can speak well in public Meetings. You do well as Leaders, Managers and Bosses.

Business and Finances

You are not so keen on building your bank balance, yet you do save money, which you are inclined to use for the benefit of the public at large. You have a strong desire to possess a second house, such as a country home.

You are fond of traveling, but one of these journeys will be the cause of financial reverses or loss in social position. You have very good relations with your servants and employees. But you should be careful that the latter do not cause you any financial harm.

You match with Gemini, Libra or Aquarius.

Romance and Marriage

Your domestic life is usually gets disturbed when you tend to lose your mental balance. Your love affairs will have a strong intellectual and artistic bias. Since you are very idealistic, you will have to be adaptable in your matrimonial relationship, even if you find that your partner does not come up to your standard. Your spouse will have an artistic temperament but is likely to be proud and imperious.

Health and Disease

You suffer from high blood pressure, hardening of arteries and Circulatory problems. Your sign rules nervous and lymphatic systems the ankles, calves of the legs, and throat, lungs, heart. You have a strong constitution, but are liable to fall ill suddenly, and such illnesses affect your nervous system. Precautions should also be taken against infectious diseases. You have a tendency to put on weight if you are not careful. You are also prone to sinus and bladder infections, varicose veins and cramps in lower legs.

YOUR WEAKNESS

Since you are over sensitive, your feelings are easily hurt. You often tend to loose control of yourself and do undesirable acts or things which you regret later. Though you are quite social yet you suffer from loneliness at times. In personal life you often indulge in lovely romantic affairs or extra marital affairs, which make your married life unhappy.

Lucky Days   Sunday, Saturday
Lucky Colors   Purple, Grey, black, blue, bluish green.
Lucky Stone   Sapphire, aquamarine, opal, onyx.
Your Lucky Numbers 4, 13, 22, 31, 40, 49.

PISCES (19th February to 20th March)

Your Planetary Ruler   Jupiter, Neptune
Your Element   Water
Your sign   Fixed

Characteristics

You will be philosophical, restless, contemplating, imagining, honest, outspoken and helpful. You will be sweet tempered and socially inclined towards others. You being a common and famine sign your expression and thoughts will be modified and even thoroughly changed when you are in front of the audience you will have the desire to study the occult science and the divine life of god.

Appearance

You are generally of short stature with a tendency to be plump, short limbs, a full face, pale complexion, a tendency to develop a double chin, muscular and spherical shoulders. You have big and protruding eyes, soft and silky hair and a wide mouth.

Personality

You have a kind, loving, truthful and sympathetic nature. Usually, you are courteous and hospitable, helpful and humane, and you cannot harm any one even if you try. Being a dual sign, you are a puzzle to others and even to yourself. By and large, you are sweet tempered and social.

Professions and Career

You can be successful as accountants, bankers, as performers in music and opera houses, cinema, practitioners of occult sciences, actors, liaison officers, personnel in medical and education departments.

Business and Finances

You have good business ability. You are end owed with skills, which will bring you wealth and power. You do not relish the idea of being dependent on your children in old age so you keep the money safe for that period. You are helpful to needy people but mostly make advances of money to those who can repay on demand. You have plurality of interests.

Romance and Marriage

You are strongly attracted to romance and look for a combination of good looks and intellect in your partner. However, you tend to be suspicious by nature towards your partner, which can kill your love. You are easily taken in by flattery, and should not select a partner who sets too much store on socialization.

Ideal Match Virgo, Cancer and Pisces.

Health and Diseases

Your mostly inclined to suffer from Nervous, Depression, Insomnia Anemia and Eye trouble.

Your Weakness

You are have the quality to speak and understand the domestic difficulties of the poor and will go about to assist them in the need of their hour but without considering your own financial position. The main weakness in you that you will rely upon all your friends and you will realize late in your life that your friends have not withstood to your expectation.

You are advised not to keep contemplating and daydreaming.

Lucky Days   Monday, Tuesday and Thursday
Lucky Colors   Yellow, and Orange
Lucky Stones   Yellow Sapphire, Opal and Ruby
Lucky Numbers 2, 11, 22, 31, 40

CHAPTER FOURTEEN

ZODIAC SIGNS IN BRIEF

ARIES - MESHA

Persons born in Aries will have a certain amount of independent thinking and reasoning faculty. Aries will be capable. Aries may not be strict followers of convention. They are lovers of scientific thought and philosophy; have their own ideas of right and wrong and are strongly bent upon educational pursuits. Aries are rather stubborn but often frank, impulsive and courageous. Aries are more gossipers than practical men. They sometimes require a certain amount of cajolery and sycophancy to raise them to action. Aries become pioneers.

As Mars is the lord of Aries, they will be martial in spirit. Their constitution will be hot, and they are occasionally subject to hot complaints, piles and the like, and must avoid enterprises obviously involving any serious risks. Aries love beauty, art and elegance.

The diseases Aries suffer from will be mostly those of the head and unpleasant sightseeing may often lead to mental affliction and derangement of brain. Their build will be slender and females generally possess fairly perfect contours. One peculiarity is craning the neck.

TAURUS

The stature of the persons born in Taurus will be medium or short and often inclined towards corpulence, lips thick, complexion swarthy, square face, well-shaped lips and dark hair are prominent features. Women in Taurus are generally handsome. They generally resemble the bull in their behavior toward new people if they are not listened to properly. They have their own principles and ways. Often they have a piercing intellect. They shine well as authors, book dealers and journalists. They are not bound by sentimentality but appreciate truth. They are remarkable for their ability to commit to memory. Physical and mental endurance of Taurus are note-worthy. They have much business knack and good intuition. They often think they are born to exercise authority over others and in a sense they are right. They are sensitive to physical influences. They are often liable to extremes, zealous and easily accessible to adulteration. They are sensitive to suffer from nervous complaints after their fiftieth year but their memory and powers of imagination will never deceive them. They are slow to anger, but when provoked, furious like the bull. Taurus are passionate and may become preys to sexual diseases in their old age unless they moderate their pleasures and learn to exercise self-control.

GEMINI

Persons when born in Gemini is rising have a wavering mind, often tall and straight in nature and active in motion, forehead broad, eyes clear and nose, a bit snub. Gemini is active and become experts in mathematical sciences; and mechanical sciences provided Saturn has some strong influence over them.

They will be "jack of all trades but master of none". Gemini are vivacious, but liable to be inconstant. They will have sudden nervous breakdowns and must exercise a certain amount of caution in moving with the opposite sex; a habit of self-control must be cultivated.

Mind of Gemini will be often conscious of their own faults. Gemini is liable to fraud and deceit will characterize their nature.

If evil planets are found in Gemini, trickery and deceit will characterize their nature. Many of these traits can be corrected by training.

CANCER

Persons born under Cancer have a middle-sized body, face full, nose snubbed to some extent and complexion white. They often have a double chin. They are very intelligent, bright and frugal and equally industrious. Their frugality often takes the form of miserliness. They are sympathetic but moral cowardice will be present. They will be much attached to their children and family. Their extreme sensitiveness renders them nervous and queer. Their minds will be bent upon schemes of trade and manufacture. They often meet with disappointments in marriage and love affairs. They are very talkative, self-reliant, honest and unbending. Cancer has reputation for love of justice and fair play. Saturn's situation in the ascendant is not desirable.

LEO

Persons born under Leo will be majestic in appearance, broad shoulders, and bilious constitution and bold and respectful in appearance. They possess the knack to adapt them to any condition of life. They are rather ambitious and sometimes avaricious too. They are independent thinkers. They stick up to orthodox principles in religion but are perfectly tolerant towards to others precepts and practices. Leo is lovers of fine arts and literature and possesses a certain amount of philosophical knowledge. They are voracious readers. If the ascendant or the tenth house is afflicted, they may not succeed in life as much as they expect. They put forth much struggle. Their ambitions remain unfulfilled to some extent unless the horoscope has certain definite Raja-Yogas. They are capable of non-attachment and contentment.

As Saturn happens to be lord of the 7th, Leo must resist the temptation of yielding much to their wives or husbands if domestic happiness is to prevail.

VIRGO

People born when Virgo is rising will exhibit their intelligence and memory when quite young. They will be middle-sized persons and exhibit taste in art and literature.

Their chest will be prominent and when afflicted, very weak also. They are discriminating and emotional and are carried away by impulses. Virgo love music and fine arts and acquire much power and influence over other people. They are liable to suffer from nervous breakdowns and paralysis when the sign is afflicted. Other combinations warranting Virgo can become great philosophers or writers. They are generally lucky in respect of their wives or husbands.

LIBRA

The complexion of persons born in Libra sign will be fair, their stature middle-sized, face broad, eyes fine, chest broad and light, appearance handsome, constitution rather phlegmatic, sensual disposition and keen observation. They have keen foresight and reason out things from the standpoint of their own views. Firm in conviction and unmoved by mean motives they are somewhat susceptible to the feelings of others' minds. They are more idealists than realists or practical men and often contemplate upon schemes like building castles in the air. Libra is not sensitive to what others say to them. But as political leaders and religious reformers they exert tremendous influence over masses and sometimes their zeal and enthusiasm goes to such a high pitch that they force their views upon others of opposite thoughts not realizing the baneful after-effects of such procedure. They love excitement and have the power of intuition upon which they often rely for their own guidance. They are not amenable to reason. Libra are great lovers of music. Libra have a special liking for truth and honesty and do not hesitate to sacrifice even their lives at the alters of freedom and fair play. Domestic life of Libra may be crossed by frequent tensions.

SCORPIO

Those born under Scorpio sign have youthful appearance, a generous disposition and fierce eyes. Scorpio are fickle minded and love much excitement. Scorpio is inclined to sensual things in reality while they will not hesitate to philosophies upon the merits of controlling sensual pleasures. Even females born in Scorpio sign will have more of masculine tendencies. They are good correspondents and invite from among people throughout the world. They can become expert musicians if they care to practice the art.

They are proficient in fine arts, dancing and the like and no doubt they have a philosophic disposition. They set at naught conventional habits and customs. They vehemently uphold their own views but nevertheless will not clash with those holding opposite ones. Constitution of Scorpio will be hot and they are liable to suffer from piles after their 30th year. They are silent and dignified and never speak before weighing each and every word. Scorpio is a good conversationalist as well

ZODIAC SIGNS IN BRIEF

as writers and often rely too much on their own intelligence. Married life of Scorpio may not be quite happy not only due to temperamental differences but also due to illness affecting the generative system of the partner, unless there are other compensating combinations.

SAGITTARIUS

Jupiter rules this sign and persons born under this sign will generally be inclined towards corpulence. Sagittarius possesses almond eyes and their hair is brown. They are of a phlegmatic temperament. Sagittarius are somewhat conventional and sometimes businesslike also. They are prompt and uphold conservative views. They will be attracted towards the study of occult philosophy and sciences. In these departments of knowledge Sagittarius can acquire mastery. They are too callous and enthusiastic. They hate all external show. Sagittarius is God-fearing, honest, humble and free from hypocrisy. They never think of schemes, which are calculated to disturb the progress of others. Sagittarius generally exercise control over their food and drinks but in regard to their relationship with the opposite sex restraint is called for. They are brilliant, their manners affable, winning and hearts, pure.

Sagittarius is prone to be misunderstood unintentionally by others on account of their hastiness in conversation. In their later years they must be careful about their lungs as they are liable to suffer from rheumatic pains and the like. Combinations for political power warranting, persons born in Sagittarius sign will exercise power with firmness and justice and without yielding to corruptive influences.

CAPRICORN

Persons born in Capricorn sign will be tall, reddish brown in color with prominent hair on the eyebrows and the chest. Women born in Capricorn will be handsome and youngish in appearance. Capricorn has large teeth and sometimes protruding outside the lips and presenting an uncouth appearance if the second house is afflicted. The lips of Capricorn are fleshy and ladies have an inviting appearance. They have the knack of adopting themselves to circumstances and environments. They have great aspirations in life and cannot economies funds even if they were to be under the influence of adversity. They are modest, liberal and gentlemanly in business transactions. Capricorn is noted for their perseverance and strong mindedness. In fact they are stoical to the miseries of life. They are possessed of sympathy, generosity and philanthropy and take great interest in literature, science and education. Sometimes they are vindictive. When Saturn is badly posited, Capricorn is possessed of bigotry. God-fearing and humble they make good husbands or wives. Depending upon the disposition of the 9th house Capricorn can become philosophically minded or develop social consciousness.

AQUARIUS

Those born under Aquarius sign will be tall, lean, fairly handsome, manners winning, appearance attractive, and disposition elegant. Lips of Aquarius are fleshy, cheeks broad with prominent temples and buttocks. They are highly intelligent and make friends of others very soon. They are peevish and when provoked, rise like a bulldog but their anger is very soon subsided. They are pure in heart and always inclined to help others. They shine very well as writers and good spokesman. They are at times timid. Aquarius feel shy to exhibit their talents but their conversation will be most interesting and highly instructive.

They will specialize in subjects like astrology, psychology and healing arts, etc. Literacy greatness of Aquarius will come before the world when they are quite young and they themselves will not be able to estimate their capacities well, while others find in them something remarkable and extraordinary. They are intuitive and good judges of character. Aquarius have no organizing capacity and are devoted to their husbands or wives and never betray the interests of even their enemies, when trust is placed in them.

Aquarius are liable to suffer from colic troubles and must take special precautions to safeguard themselves against diseases incidental to exposure to cold weather. On the whole Aquarius people have something subtle in them, which endears them to all they come in contact with.

PISCES

Persons born in Pisces sign will be fair, stout and moderately tall. Pisces are reserved in their manners and are liable to draw premature conclusions on any matter. They are God-fearing. Pisces are generally superstitious and religious, rigid in the observance of orthodox principles and can forego anything but their orthodoxy; or they can be exactly the opposite. They are somewhat stubborn, rather timid, and ambitious to exercise authority over others. They are true friends and are proud of their educational and other attainments. If the lord of the 7th is badly afflicted, Pisces will have double marriage. They are restless and fond of history, antiquarian talks and mythological masterpieces. Pisces are frugal in spending money and though generally dependent upon others thorough out their life still bear a mark of independence. Pisces are just in their dealings and fear to transgress the laws of truth. With all this, they lack self-confidence.

CHAPTER FIFTEEN

AFFLICTION OF VARIOUS PLANETS

AFFLICTION OF SUN

The affliction of sun can lead to headaches, fevers, pain in bones, and lack of energy.

AFFLICTION OF MOON

The affliction of moon indicates mental illness, and can be a cause of blood pressure, cough and diseases of chest.

AFFLICTION OF MARS

The affliction of Mars can cause boils, blood cancer, bone marrow, as well as menstrual disorder in ladies.

AFFLICTION OF RAHU

The affliction of Rahu is responsible for smallpox, sleeplessness, delusions, varicose veins and leprosy.

AFFLICTION OF JUPITER

The affliction of Jupiter can be the cause of Diabetes, jaundice, and flatulence.

AFFLICTION OF SATURN

The affliction of Saturn denotes Arthritis, pain in knees and legs as well as diseases like tumours, paralysis and bone fractures.

AFFLICTION OF MERCERY

The affliction of Mercury can cause skin problems, diseases of nerves, epilepsy and leucoderma.

AFFLICTION OF KETU

The affliction of Ketu can lead to situation where surgery becomes imperative. It also indicates the root of wounds caused through accidents and skin eruptions apart from speech defects and phobias.

AFFLICTION OF VENUS

The affliction of Venus can lead to impotency, problem in the ovaries, barrenness and drug abuse or addiction.

CHAPTER SIXTEEN

COMPATABILITY OF ZODIAC SIGNS

ARIES WITH OTHER ZODIAC SIGNS

ARIES WITH ARIES

An Aries female tends to dominate and if one person will submit to the other there should be much compatibility between two persons born in this fire sign. If both Arians have dominant and forceful aspects in their horoscopes, conflict will arise, as both partners desire to be head of the family. The situation dictates that both shall go for their own careers or directions independently. What starts out so promisingly ends in disharmony? A divorce can be rather be violent and heart breaking.

There in order to lead a happy and peaceful life they both have to submit to each other their likes and dislikes.

ARIES WITH TAURUS

Aries is impulsive, but Taurus is steady. Both are highly sensual, but the deliberate teasing and unpredictable lovemaking of Taurus can annoy Aries. Taurus is possessive and views Aries's need to be an individual desire rather than individual demand. Taurus is good at earning money but Aries is more spend thrift. This match may not make a fine combination as Venus, the goddess of love, rules Taurus nature and Mars the fiery planet rules Aries. Taurus being slow moving may find the going a bit hectic, though excitement may help to stimulate the friendship but this friendship may not be a lasting affair. Arians tend to omit their temperamental outbursts. Taurus is not highly emotional on the surface, but they can become furious as a bull, as and when they see red in Aries.

ARIES WITH GEMINI

They won't bore each other because as both love to talk more. Gemini is versatile and ingenious and Aries is dynamic and intelligent. They share a special compatibility, for Gemini is as restless and anxious to try new things as Aries is. Gemini is clever enough to counter Aries's needs. The signals are definitely go. Aries is likely to be the leader sexually, and Gemini delights in thinking up variations to keep Aries's interest at a peak. Gemini being a mercurial sign, where the mind plays an important part in all love making, and the emotional Arian may be too much for the conventional nature of the Gemini. This combination sometimes has a great deal of hankering because of strong differences in their personalities. It is not a great match up.

ARIES WITH CANCER

These two are fascinated with each other. Cancer is cautious. Cancer loves heart and home and Aries hates to be tied down. Resentments often build up and they argue over petty mattes. Aries has a sharp tongue that wounds the Cancers. This combination is usually hard to match. The moon rules Cancers, making them moody, sentimental and secretive. Their tendency is to live in the past, and they have a difficult time forgetting serious quarrels or disagreement that may occur occasionally this is quite true of this couple.

ARIES WITH LEO

This is usually a great combination. But both have got egos problems and both like to lead. Aries wouldn't dream of taking second place, and Leo needs constant watch. They can work it out properly if neither tries to defame the other. Though it's a fine sexual match, as both are fiery and romantic. Aries is optimistic and open to life; Leo is generous and good-hearted. They could find room to compromise easily as with both sides being emotional in their make up, Leo will fascinate an Arian mate if Aries will allow Leo to hold the centre of the floor on occasions. Their sex life could be legendary and infidelity kept to a minimum, or eliminated all together if each of them find what they want from each other, and not have a physical compulsion to stray. Leo admires the aggressive tendencies of fiery signs. That is why Arians make this an ideal union.

ARIES WITH VIRGO

Mercury rules Virgo and Aries are ruled by Mars. But they have totally different ideas. Aries's passions are impulsive and direct. Virgo's sexuality is more enigmatic and takes time to be revealed. In other areas Aries is full of exciting new plans and ideas, and insists on being boss. Virgo is critical and fussy, and likes things to be done the way he wants. They end up making war, not love and do not blend well astrologically. Virgos desire a well-ordered existence and won't be happy under Arian leadership. If the Arian allows Virgo space, and acknowledges the virtues of Virgo, the two can make for a dynamic relationship.

ARIES WITH LIBRA

Libra wants peace, quiet, and harmony while Aries wants action and adventure. Both like social life, entertaining, and pleasure, but both are restless in their ways. There is a powerful initial attraction between these two but their love life may be bit unconventional. Libra will look for someone less demanding, and Aries will bind someone for more dictating.

Marvellous affair but poor marriage shows. Libra's refined and artistic temperament wishes for reciprocal attachments. And this is something Aries cannot provide. There is a wider the ordinary margin for error though, and most of these combinations will go at the distance and nonreciprocal.

ARIES WITH SCORPIO

With Mars dominating both signs it makes for very positive temperaments unless there are some bad natal planetary aspects. Since Aries won't take orders from Scorpions and Scorpio will never take a back seat. Love cannot be a bonfire between these two. Though they've physical, energetic, and passionate in their sexual nature and each has a forceful personality and wants to control the other there is no room for these two. This combination is can make an ideal match if one ignores to dominate the other.

ARIES WITH SAGITTARIUS

The Mars-Jupiter duo is usually an ideal match for each other. Sagittarius is a perfect ideal and temperamental match for Aries. They both are active, spontaneous people. There may be a little conflict because both are impulsive and brutally frank. However, they have wonderful senses of humor and enjoy each other's company. If they make it in the bedroom, they'll make it everywhere else. Most people of these matches are in it for life. The Sagittarius means liberty, and the pursuit of happiness while Aries is subscribes to this theory. And for this reason, that makes them a good match

ARIES WITH CAPRICORN

Capricorns are usually patient and are traditionally easygoing. Arians are too impatient to cope with the slowness attitude. Saturn represents the Capricorn and Mars governs the Aries. Aries's taste for innovation and experiment may not please Capricorns. Aries is restless, fiery, and impulsive; Capricorn is ordered, settled, and practical. Capricorn needs to dominate and so does Aries. Problems often crops up over moneymaking schemes. Not a hopeful combination. Capricorn will nod against the Arian will and a disagreement is bound to occur. In the matter of sex there is an affinity; however, their inherent personalities clash. The combination of a fire sign with an earth sign. Aries is a fiery in nature while Capricorn is earth, cautious and reserved. Aries prefers to take action while Capricorn would rather plan and wait. Without a great deal of tolerance and patience, there is not much hope for this union.

ARIES WITH AQUARIUS

Both signs are of independent nature but at times Aquarius will do things without notice with which Aries may become impatient. Since both are active, ambitious, enjoy a wide range of interests, and are equally eager for sexual adventure. As both are independent Aquarius energies more than Aries and Aries may at times feel neglected. Aries finds the Aquarian unpredictability exciting, but feels entirely insecure. However, with a bit of tact and understanding on both sides, this is a great affair that could turn into something even better. This could possibly be a good relationship, but will require a positive attitude on both parts.

ARIES WITH PISCES

Pisceans are romantic and they desire the delicate approach that which the Arian lacks. Aries will draw Pisces out of their shell, and in turn will be appealed by Pisces mysterious nature in terms of sexuality. The boldness and confidence of Aries adding to the Pisces's intuitions and fantasies end in an eventful union. Pisces is somewhat shy and Aries likes to be dominant, Pisces likes having someone to be looked upon. For a happy coupling thus requires only a little more tact on Ariean part.

TAURUS WITH OTHER ZODIAC SIGNS

TAURUS WITH ARIES

Taurus is possessive and views Aries's need to be an individual desire rather than individual demand. Aries is an impatient, energetic sign, rather domineering the slower-moving Taurus may find the going a bit hectic, but the excitement may help stimulate courtship since Taurus is a highly emotional sign, though very obstinate when dictated to. Taurean nature is ruled by Venus, the goddess of love, and Aries is ruled by Mars the fiery planet. Aries is impulsive, but Taurus is steady. Both are highly sensual, but the deliberate teasing and unpredictable lovemaking of Taurus can annoy Aries. This match may not make a fine combination as Taurus being slow moving may find the going a bit hectic, though excitement may help to stimulate the friendship but this friendship may not be a lasting affair.

TAURUS WITH TAURUS

Both are earthy creatures that prefer safety to adventure. From a physical stand point; this appears to be a compatible combination. Both share a fondness for money, and are hardworking, loyal, and affectionate.

The female Taurean tends to be more sentimental than the male Taurean, but each is as possessive than the other, which works out fine. Because they are both earthy and direct about sexual needs, there should be no problem in that department, if one adheres to the will and wishes of the other.

TAURUS WITH GEMINI

The Gemini personality may prove to be too restless for the Taurus nature. The two signs are emotionally at distance. These two are completely unalike in temperament. Taurus is fixed in opinions, resistant to change. Gemini is restless, vacillating. Gemini is attracted to Taurus's passions, but in time Taurus's instinct for security and stability will be offended by Gemini volatile nature. Taurus's demands are simply too much for Gemini, who seeks excuses. Taurus with the innate need to possess will never be able to hang on to the unsettled Gemini. Gemini loves change and Taurus resists it so becomes rather difficult for both of them to come to an understanding in the matters of making love.

TAURUS WITH CANCER

Usually this makes a good combination. Cancer likes a good home with much affection. This is what every Taurean hopes to find when undertaking conventional responsibilities. Cancer needs someone like Taurus to depend on as Cancer gives Taurus the loyalty and feedback it needs. Taurus is ambitious for money and security, and Cancer has exactly those same goals. Similar interests and desires make for harmonious meetings. From an emotional point of view, there is nothing in the stars that bars the prospect of a happy married life between these two partners. This is a good combination as both signs are naturally attracted by the others sense for feelings and emotions.

TAURUS WITH LEO

Venus and the Sun make a good combination, especially when each understands the other's faults. Excellent physical qualities and great attraction is there for both partners. Taurus will supply the attention that Leo requires but will expect it to be returned. A strong attraction physically and emotionally but having too many obstacles to cope with.

TAURUS WITH VIRGO

With both being earth signs there will be much common ground for these two. Both Virgo and Taurus desire material success and security. Taurus keeps a careful eye on expenditures, which pleases Virgo. Although they lack what might be called a spontaneous approach to life, neither puts a high value on that. Both share the same intellectual pursuits. Taurus's attraction and Virgo's sharp mind are a good combination for success as a team.

TAURUS WITH LIBRA

Libra an air sign loves to roam and Taurus an earth sign loves to sit and waits patiently. With understanding it could be a harmonic relationship. Taurus balances Libra's indecisiveness. Taurus finds Libra a warm, romantic, partner. Libra is born to charm. The love goddess and it does shine on the two lovebirds that are until one-steps out of line. Both signs are ruled by Venus and have sensual natures, but each expresses this quality differently. However there are common interest and a meeting of the mind and body making this a very good marital combination. They appreciate beauty and the finer things of life.

TAURUS WITH SCORPIO

These two are opposites in the zodiac, but they have more in common than other opposites. Both are determined and ambitious, and neither is much of a lover. These are zodiac opposites, but they are compatible earth and water signs. This usually manifests itself in a strong physical attraction. This combination mutually admires each other. Jealousy however is the big problem with this pair and that seems to be always showing its face. Taurus must be careful to keep faith with the scorpion, or else this combination will fall down without warning.

TAURUS WITH SAGITTARIUS

These are two very different personality types the more reserved Taurus and the outgoing Sagittarius both has an appreciation for the truth. Sagittarius has an easy live and let live attitude this might work if Taurus can tie a string to Sagittarius's.

The Taurus who marries a Sagittarian will find that no amount of arguing or berating is going to change the reckless Sagittarian With some understanding they can find harmony in their characters as long as they allow each other their personalities. With the Taurean being possessive and the Sagittarian being freedom loving, the Sagittarian may find this hard to co-operate with.

TAURUS WITH CAPRICORN

A good combination of the basic earth signs. Both are responsible and practical natures. They even have a mutual desire for success and material things. Capricorn is a strong match for Taurus, for they both have passions that are straightforward and uncomplicated. Capricorn is a bit more secretive than Taurus. With both partners having mutual understanding of each other's personalities this can be a very compatible marriage. Venus and Saturn blend very well from an emotional point of view.

TAURUS WITH AQUARIUS

These two live on opposite sides of the planet, in fact some times, Taurus will wonder if Aquarius is even from this planet. Neither is likely to approve of the other. Taurus is conservative, careful, closemouthed. Aquarius is unconventional, innovative, and vivacious. Taurus is lusty and passionate while Taurus needs security and comfort. Aquarius, a fancy-free loner who resents ties that bind. This combination heads in for many difficulties. The Aquarian being unpredictable both love ease and comfort but their views on how to obtain them are very different. Another big irritation for the Taurus lover is the unwillingness of the Aquarius to share his secrets. Aquarius will find the Taurus attention somewhat smothering and restrictive.

TAURUS WITH PISCES

These two can share a great deal of their appreciation for beauty, art, and sensuality and just about any of the finer things in life. Pisces may not altogether understand Taurus's materialistic approach to life. Taurus's practical, easygoing nature helps Pisces through its frequent changes of mood.

In love, Taurus is devoted and Pisces adores. This usually is a very happy combination. Pisces being romantic, imaginative, impressionable and flexible is just what the Taurus native is looking for.

GEMINI WITH OTHER ZODIAC SIGNS

GEMINI WITH ARIES

Gemini respects the refined, intellectual approach to continual bliss. Impatient Arians may find this frustrating, after awhile may try to find a less difficult companion. This lively, energetic pair can be good friends as well as good lovers. Aries will probably make the decisions because Gemini has difficulty in that area. Not a great match up, but can work with understanding and effort. Aries needs to calm down. Don't get me wrong. Gemini is versatile and ingenious and Aries is dynamic and intelligent. They share a special compatibility, for Gemini is as restless and anxious to try new things as Aries is. Gemini is clever enough to counter Aries's needs. Gemini being a mercurial sign, where the mind plays an important part in all love making, and the emotional Arian may be too much for the conventional nature of the Gemini. It is not a great match up.

GEMINI WITH TAURUS

The Gemini personality may prove to be restless for the Taurean nature. Taurus wants life to be stables and ordered, while Gemini is easily bored and looks for new experiences. These two are completely unalike in temperament. Taurus's demands are simply and Gemini seeks excuses. Gemini loves change and Taurus resists it so becomes rather difficult for both of them to come to an understanding in the matters of understanding each other. An unpromising match.

GEMINI WITH GEMINI

As both are of air signs and are ruled by the planet mercury. These two will never bore each other, for they are interested in everything. A compatible combination this should prove to be, at least both would understand each other's changeable nature. The Gemini demands for change and variety will keep this relationship some how moving. Whether it produces a happiness or sadness depends on at least one of the companion paying attention, at least for some time. Discussions will be lively and ever changing life may become restless but again they cannot have it in any other way.

GEMINI WITH CANCER

Cancer needs security and homely atmosphere whereas Gemini dislikes to be being tied down. These two have too little in common for a long-term relationship. Gemini lacks patience with Cancer's moods and Gemini's sharp tongue is too harsh for Cancer's strong ego. While Gemini is constantly on the alert for change, Cancer is satisfied to become a truly homely mate. Cancers are driven by emotion and feelings and generally prefer to be constant. Gemini's unstoppable movement may prove be unsettling to Cancer's needs. They are poised for a downward trend. Gemini makes Cancer feel quite insecure and their affair is likely to result in a volatile behaviour.

GEMINI WITH LEO

On the surface there is great mutual attraction for both signs. While Leo loves with his heart first, Gemini loves with his mind.

Both are naturally attracted to glamour and flattery of the world. Their affair is a chase after variety and amusement. An affectionate pair who really enjoy each other. Leo will probably demand more adoration than

Gemini is willing to give. Socially, each tries to upstage the other, but they have a lot of fun together doing it. There is good reason to be optimistic about this pairing; all in all this is a very good combination of air and fire.

GEMINI WITH VIRGO

Both are Mercury-ruled and have a mental approach to life. They are attracted to each other because of a mutual interest in intellectual ideas. Both have active minds. Virgo's analytical approach seems like indifference to Gemini. Virgo looks on Gemini's busy social life as superficial and a waste of time. Virgo is critical; Gemini is tactless. Mercury is calculating and logical; in Virgo it is critical and demanding. Gemini's ever-present desire for change would be much for the realistic Virgo. One point for the two to be compatible would be the desire for good clothes, cleanliness, mutual desire for friends and associates who are engaged in intellectual and artistic pursuits. Gemini can deal with Virgo's critical eye, well, this could work.

GEMINI WITH LIBRA

These two air signs are well suited in every way. Both signs have much in common and enough to make an ideal partnership. Libra being under Venus's influence and Mercury ruling Gemini makes for a very good planetary combination. This will be a very stimulating relationship. One sign compliments the other and brings out the better part of each other's nature. Gemini will find it easy to communicate with Libra who is only too happy to share his information and ideas. They are affectionate, fun loving, entertaining, and travel fond. This is considered to be a great astrological influence for a long and happy marriage.

GEMINI WITH SCORPIO

An air sign with a water sign. Gemini is too changeable and inconstant for intense Scorpio, who needs and demands total commitment. Scorpio is basically a loner; Gemini likes to glitter in social settings.

Gemini has a strong penchant for independence, while Scorpio wants to dominate and possess. Gemini's desire for freedom of action will clash with the jealous and possessive nature of Scorpio. While some Gemini-Scorpio combinations may work out fairly well, the pure Gemini- Scorpio alliance packs as much power as an atomic bomb. These two will have some difficulty rectifying their innate natures. Love conquers all. Then again, too much, stifles some. These two are opposites in the zodiac and are attracted to each other like magnets. They'll especially enjoy each other's minds for both have wide-ranging and varied interests.

GEMINI WITH SAGITTARIUS

Gemini is ruled by Mercury and Sagittarius is ruled by Jupiter the planet of knowledge and wisdom. Both have bright minds, but Sagittarius is outspoken while Gemini likes to enjoy fun. They are usually a compatible combination with both being frank, outspoken, and a certain amount of personal understanding being made. They meet on a common ground, and can plan their lives with equilibrium. They are restless, adventuresome, imaginative, and fun loving. No other opposite signs in the zodiac enjoy each other more than these two. However if Sagittarius forgoes its ego and Gemini restores to concrete planning they can make a good combination otherwise their combination may not last long.

GEMINI WITH CAPRICORN

Capricorn gets worried about security, while Gemini feels about losing its liberty. The Saturn ruled Capricorn will be at differences with the Mercury ruled Gemini. Patience is a virtue with Capricorn, but it is not so with Gemini. Gemini's need for a survival does nothing to make Capricorn feel secure. Gemini's free talks, meets opposition from conservative Capricorn. Capricorn's great drive to execute will prove to be too much for the Gemini. Until they both are ready to minimize their goals. Capricorn will go on hunting until he gains the upper hand. Of course with these two people going together anything is possible and the outcome of the result may not be satisfying to each other.

GEMINI WITH AQUARIUS

Gemini is bit inconstant or unstable, Aquarius understands somewhat Gemini's needs. Gemini is always looking for surprises and the Aquarian can give them. Gemini and Aquarius get along quite easily. They share a taste for new things, travelling, meeting new people and doing new things. Since both are unpredictable, things may always go smoothly with them. But love keeps getting them together, for Aquarius adores Gemini's wit and good cheer. The caring, thoughts of Aquarius will find a smooth home with Gemini. Uranus, the ruling planet of Aquarius, is full of surprises and sudden changes. This will suit the Gemini perfectly. There will be plenty of none stop variety to afford the stimulation that Gemini needs for its dual personality and goal.

GEMINI WITH PISCES

Their passion is quite high, and so are their problems. Pisces get easily hurt by thoughtless Gemini. Gemini is mischievous and playful, but Pisces is sensitive and takes things to heart easily. Each practices in his or her thoughts in their own way: Gemini needs freedom and Pisces needs unending appreciation. Pisces just can't feel secure with talkative moods of Gemini, and he tries to pull the net in his own way. This atmosphere eventually makes it hard for Gemini to breathe his own liberty. The freedom of Gemini is stake if he marries a Piscean. Gemini's should be prepared to change their ways if they want to seek happiness with a loving and possessive Piscean.

CANCER WITH OTHER ZODIAC SIGNS

CANCER AND ARIES

The moon rules Cancer, making him moody, sentimental and secretive. Aries is ruled by mars and makes him bold and aggressive. Cancer is easily hurt by Aries's aggressiveness and sharp tongue. Cancer likes security and Aries needs freedom to explore new worlds. Both like to accumulate money. Aries wants to spend it and Cancer wants to keep it. Too many problems here. This combination is usually hard to match. Cancer holds on like that of a crab, while Aries cannot part with the things so easily that are with them. The secretive nature of Cancer has the potential of clashing with the openness of Aries. Though Aries can be moody too, it is not quite so bad as Cancer. If they make it through the first year or so the rest may turn out to be an easy affair.

CANCER AND TAURUS

This is a good combination as both signs are naturally attracted to each other. Both need security and both are loving, affectionate, and passionate. Both are moneymakers, and together they enjoy the delights of heart and home. Taurus is good for Cancer's moodiness. What each needs the other supplies?

From an emotional point of view, there is nothing in the stars that bars the prospect of a happy married life between these two partners. One thing is what Tureen should remember is that Cancer is sensitive, and will crawl into a shell if he or she is unhappy emotionally.

CANCER AND GEMINI

Gemini is constantly on the alert for change, Cancer is satisfied to become a true mate. Cancer's nature is emotional and Gemini's nature is openness and that makes it difficult for them to understand each other. Cancer will try to keep Gemini penned in, and Gemini can't abide that. Cancer and moodiness may become too much for Gemini to cope with. There would be better compatibility where the female is a Gemini and the male is a Cancerian, Cancers are driven by emotion and feelings and generally prefer to remain constant while Gemini's unstoppable movement and talkative nature will prove unpleasant to Cancer desire.

CANCER AND CANCER

They understand each other perfectly and can also wound each other without even trying hard or harsh. Both are too sensitive, demanding and dependent. They have a lot in common, and each needs an enormous amount of attention. That's the main drawback and trouble. This combination can make married life easy going, because each will have a sympathetic understanding for the other's moods, and wishes. Though there are times were they may disagree, with each clinging to their previous experience and teachings each will no doubt understand the other better. Both will give enough consideration to their company and they should have no trouble in finding constant happiness.

CANCER AND LEO

Usually this is a good combination, since the Cancer reflects the light of the Leo. Leo's heart will soon forgive the mood outbursts that Cancer shows from time to time. Leo will appreciate cancer's attention and as long as cancer can forgive and forget that they feel neglected at times. Cancer will feel a bit more enthused around Leo and will probably let Leo run things.

Cancer has to get used to Leo's generous, open heartedness. Leo is just what insecure Cancer is looking for. Cancer's marvelous intuitions tell it exactly how to handle this Leo.

CANCER AND VIRGO

Virgo's demands may be a bit much for Cancer's desire for peace and quiet. Cancer's response is emotive while Virgo's is analytical. Cancer may have to warm up Virgo a little, since there is fire under the ice. This can turn into a comfortable, and affectionate relationship. Cancer's struggle for financial security works perfectly with Virgo. Cancer's dependency neatly complements Virgo's need to protect, and each is anxious to please the other. The full, affectionate feelings of cancer will not be completely satisfied by Virgo's direct approach to the practical matters at hand. Virgo will appreciate the loyalty and sincerity of cancer, but will need to be a little more demonstrative and affectionate with cancer.

CANCER AND LIBRA

Cancer is not temperamentally suited to cope with the freedom loving Libran. This pair operates on entirely different levels. Cancer is too temperamental and possessive for airy Libra. They both love a beautiful home, but Libra also needs parties and people and outside pleasures. When Cancer turns critical, especially about Libra's extravagance, Libra starts looking elsewhere. On the positive side though, they could make it. Ruled by the Moon and Venus respectively, there is common ground here despite the fact that we have a water sign and an air. Libra will appreciate Cancer's loyalty and generosity. Cancer wants love Libra seeks perfect intellectual communion.

CANCER AND SCORPIO

Water signs rule both. Cancer is loyal; Scorpio's jealousy isn't provoked. Cancer admires Scorpio's strength while Scorpio finds a haven in Cancer's emotional commitment. Both are extremely intuitive and sense what will please the other. Together they can build a happy home where they feel safe and loved. This relationship has great intimacy, intensity, and depth. Things just get better all the time. Scorpio should make a good mate for quiet spoken cancer. Scorpio and cancer could well prove the ideal marriage combination.

CANCER AND SAGITTARIUS

A water and fire combination. Sagittarius likes to wander, while Cancer is a prefers to stay at home. Cancer's commitment to total togetherness only makes Sagittarius desperate to get away. In addition, outspoken Sagittarius's bluntness continually wounds sensitive Cancer. They happen to be better friends than lovers. There is a vast difference in natures and the likely hood of being compatible is all but impossible, unless there are some positive aspects in their charts. Cancer is too needy for Sagittarius. On the good side, they are both generous people.

CANCER AND CAPRICORN

Both signs have plenty in common. Capricorn has too many other interests to give Cancer all the attention it needs. Cancer is shy, sensitive, and needs affection, while Capricorn is aloof, and domineering. Capricorn has the ability to make cancer's dream come true, while Cancer is happy wishing for and wanting the success and security that the Capricorn strives for. The elements of water and earth go well together but these are zodiac opposites you can expect both side of the coin. They will have to take the good with the bad and there will be plenty of both. Capricorn lacks the warmth and sentiment that Cancer requires.

CANCER AND AQUARIUS

Cancer has a conservative taste while Aquarius taste is usually the opposite. Aquarius is quick-minded, unpredictable, and apt to be impatient with cautious, hesitant Cancer. Cancer needs to feel close and secure. The social side of the Aquarian may prove to be too much for the Cancer. Aquarian's love to share their life stories with the world while cancer is satisfied to concentrate on personal obligations. Odds against this combination are too great for this combination, unless one will become convergent to the other. Aquarius has a need to be independent and often appears detached in a close relationship with cancer.

CANCER AND PISCES

A harmonious match and quite a perfect match as both are ruled by the water signs.

The sentimental combination of these two signs make for an ideal marriage. Although both will have their moments of gloom and doom, they will soon come out in the sunshine to forgive and forget each other. They are both romantic, need to love and be loved and can probably communicate to each other without speaking or making facial gestures. Both are emotional, intensely devoted, and sensitive to each other's moods.

LEO WITH OTHER ZODIAC SIGNS

LEO WITH ARIES

This is usually a great combination. But both have got egos problems and both like to lead. Aries wouldn't dream of taking second place, and Leo needs constant watch. They can work it out properly if neither tries to defame the other. Though it's a fine sexual match, as both are fiery and romantic. Aries is optimistic and open to life; Leo is generous and good-hearted. Leo admires the aggressive tendencies of fiery signs. That is why Arians make this an ideal union.

LEO WITH TAURUS

Leo requires but will expect it to be returned. Leo loves to dominate and eventually Taurus being strong willed but more patient.

Venus and the Sun make a good combination, especially when each understands the other's faults. Excellent physical qualities and great attraction is there for both partners. Taurus will supply the attention that Leo requires but will expect it to be returned. A strong attraction physically and emotionally but having too many obstacles to cope with.

LEO WITH GEMINI

On the surface there is great mutual attraction for both signs. While Leo loves with his heart first, Gemini loves

142

with his mind. Both are naturally attracted to glamour and flattery of the world. Their affair is a chase after variety and amusement. An affectionate pair who really enjoy each other. Leo will probably demand more adoration than Gemini is willing to give. Socially, each tries to upstage the other, but they have a lot of fun together doing it. There is good reason to be optimistic about this pairing; all in all this is a very good combination of air and fire. All in all this is a very good combination of air and fire.

LEO WITH CANCER

This is a combination of fire and water. Usually this is a good combination, since the Cancer reflects the light of the Leo. Leo's heart will soon forgive the mood outbursts that Cancer shows from time to time. Leo will appreciate cancer's attention and as long as cancer can forgive and forget that they feel neglected at times. Cancer will feel a bit more enthused around Leo and will probably let Leo run things. Cancer has to get used to Leo's generous, open heartedness. Leo is just what insecure Cancer is looking for. Cancer's marvellous intuitions tell it exactly how to handle this Leo.

LEO WITH LEO

The both being fire signs. Two positive and strong willed individuals. Both are romantic, colourful, and exuberant about life. Each not only wants to sit on the throne, each wants to be the power behind it as well. They want to be the head of their social groups. The two are constantly competing for leadership; unhappy results can result from this. The only hope for a successful partnership is for the female to be content to rule the home and the male to shine in the business and social world.

It's difficult for one Leo to make room for another ego as large as its own, but that's exactly what's needed here.

LEO WITH VIRGO

Leo being a fire sign and Virgo being the earth sign. Here is a good chance for a happy partnership. Virgo is practical Leo is extravagant and a spendthrift. Leo likes to live life in a really big way, but Virgo is conservative. This is one of those relationships that depend on the type of relationship it is. Leo will overwhelm Virgo, whose criticism will irk Leo. In business it is best when Leo leads and Virgo follows and the differences will be tolerated. Both of them should look elsewhere. If Virgo will permit Leo to hold the limelight and refrain from being too critical they should have no real barriers to a happy and successful partnership. But this may be quite hard.

LEO WITH LIBRA

Leo being a fire and Libra being an air sign. The comparability of this two shall be tiring affair. The hale and hearty Leo may prove to be too much for the sensitive Libra nature, though they have a lot in common that could make for a good combination. The sun ruling Leo and Venus ruling Libra usually form a strong and luxurious aspect. Libra is indecisive and Leo will naturally take charge. Both signs love luxuries, are subject to flattery, and are very artistically inclined. The book may not always balance because they're both extravagant and love a beautiful setting in which to shine. Each will also try to outdo the other in order to get attention.

LEO WITH SCORPIO

Leo being a fire sign and Scorpio being water sign. Two very strong willed individuals generally create some rather stormy moments. But Leo finds it hard to cope with Scorpio's jealousy and possessiveness. Scorpio considers Leo a showpiece. Scorpio doesn't understand Leo's need to be continually surrounded by an admiring audience. Scorpio would rather dominate than admire, and that doesn't suit Leo's kingly state. Two shinning personalities join together. Basically this should make for one of the most compatible combinations, but long and happy partnership will be far better a Leo female marries a Scorpio male.

LEO WITH SAGITTARIUS

Both being of fire sign. The pendulum can swing in any body's favour. Together they share a liking for freedom, adventure, and meeting new people. Leo's natural quality of leadership brings out what loyalty Sagittarius can give. Leo is very proud, but self-confident and expansive Sagittarius is quite happy to let Leo go. Both love change and excitement and have a great zest for life.

LEO WITH CAPRICORN

Leo being a fire sign whereas Capricorn is an earth sign. The combination of these two may at time lead to severe complications. The slow Capricorn may prove to be too much for the carefree nature of Leo. Leo will think Capricorn stingy with affection because Capricorn's reserved, undemonstrative nature cannot give Leo the adoration it needs. Neither will take a back seat nor let the other dominate. This affair will be on the rocks before it even leaves the dock. Leo forgives and forgets; Capricorn being the one who is slow to anger and seldom forgets. This pair would not form the ideal basis for mutual understanding. Leo likes to live for the moment and Capricorn prefers to make calculated movements.

LEO WITH AQUARIUS

Leo is a fire sign and Aquarius is an air sign. The comparability of this two in terms of worldly affairs can often become difficult to match. Both like socializing and meeting new people, but Leo always needs to perform on center stage, which makes Aquarius impatient and irritable. Aquarius is too independent to become Leo's devoted subject. And that's where it ends. Leo views Aquarius's aloof emotions as a personal rejection. Both signs are better when doing things for others. Leo loves the world and Aquarius loves humanity. This makes for an excellent combination for a partnership that deals with or caters to the public. Each has a mutual understanding of the other when it comes to intimate matters, needs and desires.

LEO WITH PISCES

A fire and water combination. Leo being a fire sign and Pisces being a water sign often makes this a unique combination. Both are more inclined to take than to give. Fiery Leo and watery Pisces. This is the depiction of these two. Generally not expected to work but both have an ability to learn from one another if they can get past their innate differences. The strong and hearty temperament of Leo may be too much for the subtle and sensitive Pisces. Pisces, with resilience, takes on the changing moods of any partnership. While Leo is flattered by the dependency of others, Pisces may be too much for Leo to take over a long period of time.

VIRGO WITH OTHER ZODIAC SIGNS

VIRGO WITH ARIES

Virgo is ruled by Mercury and Aries is ruled by Mars. But they have totally different ideas. Aries's passions are impulsive and direct. Virgo's sexuality is more enigmatic and takes time to be revealed. In other areas Aries is full of exciting new plans and ideas, and insists on being boss. Virgo is critical and fussy, and likes things to be done the way he wants. They end up making war, not love and do not blend well astrologically. Virgos desire a well-ordered existence and won't be happy under Arian leadership. If the Arian allows Virgo space, and acknowledges the virtues of Virgo, the two can make for a dynamic relationship.

VIRGO WITH TAURUS

With both being earth signs there will be much common ground for these two. Both Virgo and Taurus desire material success and security. Taurus keeps a careful eye on expenditures, which pleases Virgo.

Although they lack what might be called a spontaneous approach to life, neither puts a high value on that. Both share the same intellectual pursuits. Taurus's attraction and Virgo's sharp mind are a good combination for success as a team. The one drawback is that Virgo is normally in control of their emotional output while Taurus thrives on deep emotion and could perhaps overwhelm Virgo.

VIRGO WITH GEMINI

Both are Mercury-ruled and have a mental approach to life. They are attracted to each other because of a mutual interest in intellectual ideas. Both have active minds. Virgo's analytical approach seems like indifference to Gemini. Virgo looks on Gemini's busy social life as superficial and a waste of time. Virgo is critical; Gemini is tactless. Mercury is calculating and logical; in Virgo it is critical and demanding. Gemini's ever-present desire for change would be much for the realistic Virgo. One point for the two to be compatible would be the desire for good clothes, cleanliness, mutual desire for friends and associates who are engaged in intellectual and artistic pursuits. Gemini can deal with Virgo's critical eye, well, this could work.

VIRGO WITH CANCER

Virgo's demands may be a bit much for Cancer's desire for peace and quiet. Cancer's response is emotive while Virgo's is analytical. Cancer may have to warm up Virgo a little, since there is fire under the ice. This can turn into a comfortable, and affectionate relationship. Cancer's struggle for financial security works perfectly with Virgo. Cancer's dependency neatly complements Virgo's need to protect, and each is anxious to please the other. The full, affectionate feelings of cancer will not be completely satisfied by Virgo's direct approach to the practical matters at hand. Virgo will appreciate the loyalty and sincerity of cancer, but will need to be a little more demonstrative and affectionate with cancer.

VIRGO WITH LEO

Virgo being the earth sign and Leo being a fire sign. Here is a good chance for a happy partnership. Virgo is practical Leo is extravagant and a spendthrift. Leo likes to live life in a really big way, but Virgo is conservative. This is one of those relationships that depend, n the type of relationship it is. Leo will overwhelm Virgo, whose criticism will irk Leo. In business it is best when Leo leads and Virgo follows and the differences will be tolerated. Both of them should look elsewhere. If Virgo will permit Leo to hold the limelight and refrain from being too critical they should have no real barriers to a happy and successful partnership. But this may be quite hard.

VIRGO WITH VIRGO

Since both being the earth signs their comparability speaks of their ego problems that they may be facing while adhering to each other's view. Each of them has to forgo their egos. All is smooth sailing as long as these perfectionists curb their instincts for finding fault. Actually, they bring out the very best in each other. They are responsible, sensitive, intelligent, and take love seriously. They also share passions of the mind, and will never bore each other. Important things. Finding anything resembling compatibility would be hard for this combination. Both have a tendency to end up with a battle of the wits with both opponents evenly matched. Each would over exaggerate the faults of the other.

VIRGO WITH LIBRA

Virgo is an earth sign and Libra is and air sign. Libra enjoys spending money, going to parties, and being the centre of attention. Virgo will try to curb and dominate Libra's fickle and outer directed nature. Virgo is reserved and practical, and Libra views this as a personal rebuff. Libra will soon drift away in search of more fun-loving companions. Libra may tap Virgo's hidden sensuality but their personalities are altogether too different for real compatibility. Another combination that would have trouble finding a good marital life. Their understanding and their married life can come to settlement provided each of the other forgoes the individual ego.

VIRGO WITH SCORPIO

Virgo belongs to the earth sign while Scorpio belongs to the water sign. The combination sometimes belongs to the mutual admiration society. If Virgo will keep from hurting Scorpio's pride, this combination will be happy and enduring. Scorpio is also possessive and fiercely loyal, which makes Virgo feel loved and protected. They also admire each other's minds. Virgo is logical, intellectual, and analytical. Scorpio is imaginative, visionary, and perceptive. Scorpio is volatile but secretive, Virgo is self-restrained and reserved. The Virgo mind is very fascinated with the mysterious and intriguing Scorpio. The only problem here is on the emotional side. If each of them keeps their emotion aside there is some hope for a longer lasting friendship.

VIRGO WITH SAGITTARIUS

Virgo is an earth sign and Sagittarius is a fire sign. Their comparability often leads to unwanted and undesired conflicts. Though both are intellectual signs but the way their minds work clashes with each other. Sagittarius is expansive and extravagant, while Virgo prefers a simple, ordered, and unpretentious life. Sagittarius's free spirit has nothing in common with hardworking Virgo. The differences here are like day and night. Not all bad but difficult to reconcile with.

VIRGO WITH CAPRICORN

Since these are two earth signs the mercury and sun combination should find mutual grounds for an agreeable partnership. A harmonious pair. Both are diligent, disciplined, and have a sense of purpose. They admire one another and take great pride in pleasing each other. Both need respect and approval and each intuitively gives the other exactly that. With these two signs there are some similarity and compatibility. They are both very exacting. This stops many areas of disagreement. They both take great pride in appearance and surroundings. They can find a friend in each other.

VIRGO WITH AQUARIUS

Virgo is an earth sign while Aquarius is an air sign. Aquarius has venturesome ideas and thinks Virgo unresponsive or cold.

A lot depends on the cultural and educational levels of the partners. Aquarius is interested in other people, causes and Virgo is cautious about emotional giving. Virgo seeks personal achievement and financial security. Aquarius is outgoing, inventive, a visionary. Virgo is reserved, prudent, and very practical about its ambitions. This couple may not even make it as friends. There is a marked difference between the two; the chances for a happy and enduring marriage are almost nil. Each has a distant quality. There is no happy medium with this combination; it is either very good or very bad.

VIRGO WITH PISCES

Pisces is fascinated by Virgo's incisive, analytical mind. Virgo, love means security and mental compatibility. Pisces is the very opposite of Virgo as opposites often are sentimental and are poles apart. It will take a great deal of patience and understanding on the part of Virgo to cope with the sentimental nature of Pisces. This is another pair of zodiac opposites that can be great at times and horrible at others times. The opposites can learn a lot about themselves from their counterparts. It will go a long way in making this combination happy.

LIBRA WITH OTHER ZODIAC SIGNS

LIBRA WITH ARIES

Libra being an air sign and is a fire sign. Libra wants peace, quiet, and harmony while Aries wants action and adventure. Both like social life, entertaining, and pleasure, but both are restless in their ways. There is a powerful initial attraction between these two but their love life may be bit unconventional. Libra will look for someone less demanding, and Aries will bind someone for more dictating. Marvellous affair but poor marriage shows. Libra's refined and artistic temperament wishes for reciprocal attachments. And this is something Aries cannot provide. There is a wider the ordinary margin for error though, and most of these combinations will go at the distance and nonreciprocal.

LIBRA WITH TAURUS

Libra an air sign loves to roam and Taurus an earth sign loves to sit and waits patiently. With understanding it could be a harmonic relationship. Taurus balances Libra's indecisiveness. Taurus finds Libra a warm, romantic, partner. Libra is born to charm. The love goddess and it does shine on the two lovebirds that are until one-steps out of line. Both signs are ruled by Venus and have sensual natures, but each expresses this quality differently. However there are common interest and a meeting of the mind and body making this a very good marital combination. They appreciate beauty and the finer things of life.

LIBRA WITH GEMINI

These two air signs are well suited in every way. Both signs have much in common and enough to make an ideal partnership. Libra being under Venus's influence and Mercury ruling Gemini makes for a very good planetary combination. This will be a very stimulating relationship. One sign compliments the other and brings out the better part of each other's nature. Gemini will find it easy to communicate with Libra who is only too happy to share his information and ideas. They are affectionate, fun loving, entertaining, and travel fond. This is considered to be a great astrological influence for a long and happy marriage.

LIBRA WITH CANCER

Cancer is not temperamentally suited to cope with the freedom loving Libran. This pair operates on entirely different levels. Cancer is too temperamental and possessive for airy Libra. They both love a beautiful home, but Libra also needs parties and people and outside pleasures. When Cancer turns critical, especially about Libra's extravagance, Libra starts looking elsewhere. On the positive side though, they could make it. Ruled by the Moon and Venus respectively, there is common ground here despite the fact that we have a water sign and an air. Libra will appreciate Cancer's loyalty and generosity. Cancer wants love Libra seeks perfect intellectual communion.

LIBRA WITH LEO

Leo being a fire and Libra being an air sign. The comparability of this two shall be tiring affair. The hale and hearty Leo may prove to be too much for the sensitive Libra nature, though they have a lot in common that could make for a good combination. The sun ruling Leo and Venus ruling

Libra usually form a strong and luxurious aspect. Libra is indecisive and Leo will naturally take charge. Both signs love luxuries, are subject to flattery, and are very artistically inclined. The book may not always balance because they're both extravagant and love a beautiful setting in which to shine. Each will also try to outdo the other in order to get attention.

LIBRA WITH VIRGO

Libra is and air sign and Virgo is an earth sign Libra enjoys spending money, going to parties, and being the centre of attention. Virgo will try to curb and dominate Libra's fickle and outer directed nature. Virgo is reserved and practical, and Libra views this as a personal rebuff. Libra will soon drift away in search of more fun-loving companions. Libra may tap Virgo's hidden sensuality but their personalities are altogether too different for real compatibility. Another combination that would have trouble finding a good marital life. Their understanding and their married life can come to settlement provided each of the other forgoes the individual ego.

LIBRA WITH LIBRA

Whereas both are air signs. They both have basically the same interests and qualities, so there would be great understanding in the relationship. The biggest problem may be unresolved conflicts, as neither wants to stir the pot when differences appear. Equally demonstrative, lively, warm, sociable, in love with beautiful things, a problem is that neither wants to face reality. Though they are charming, peace loving, and adaptable, each needs a stronger balance than the other can provide. Also, because they are so much alike. Here is a match made in heaven, unless one had an incompatible sign rising at birth. While both like to be admired. With this combination there is so much in common and so little negatives

LIBRA WITH SCORPIO

Libra is an air sign where as Scorpio is a water sign. Libra may find Scorpio's intense nature a bit overwhelming. Common goals and shared interests could avert any difficulties. There is much sympathetic magnetism between these two signs. While Scorpio is the more dominating sign of the two. There is much to recommend this union, for they have many sympathies in common. Librans are sentimental and susceptible as lovers. This seems to be appealing to Scorpio's dominant and possessive urges. Scorpio is also touchy, moody, and quick to lash out in anger, which is just the kind of person Libra cannot bear. Scorpio seethes and becomes steadily more jealous and demanding, Libra has either to submit or to leave.

LIBRA WITH SAGITTARIUS

Libra being an air sign while Sagittarius being a fire sign. Their comparability is often marked by ego problems if one is able to forgo his/her ego this match can become a lasting affair. They will do well together, if Sagittarius can manage to be around enough to fulfil Libra's need for togetherness. Libra is stimulated by Sagittarius's eagerness for adventure, and Sagittarius is drawn to Libra's affectionate charm. Both are highly romantic, though this quality is more dominant in Libra. Libra will want to settle down before flighty Sagittarius does, but they can work that out. Charming, clever Libra knows how to appeal to Sagittarius's intellectual side and easily keeps Sagittarius intrigued. Sagittarius hates bondage and cannot be confined, and will not tolerate bondage, whether it be legal or not, and will use all the means at his command to break through bonds.

LIBRA WITH CAPRICORN

Libra is an air sign whereas Capricorn is an earth sign. Capricorn believes in hard work and achievement at any price. Libra is fond of socializing and nightlife, while Capricorn tends to be a loner, comfortable with only a chosen few. Libra needs flattery and attention, but Capricorn keeps its affections buried. Capricorn. And Libra's lazy, easygoing ways will offend. On the surface these two seem to be on the opposite, but the Capricorn is very much influenced by Libra. If Libra does not find the steady Capricorn nature too boring, there is good chance here for a successful marriage. Libra had better screen the social environment to suit Capricorn's views or there may be some embarrassing moments later on. Unless Capricorn can open up a little more there could be problems here. Libra requires affection and Capricorn tends to put it off.

LIBRA WITH AQUARIUS

Since both belongs to the Air signs, their comparability can said to be lasting affair. This could be a good combination for marriage. And these two have all the makings for a beautiful friendship: harmonious vibes in socializing, artistic interests, even in involvement in public affairs. Indecisive Libra is delighted with the fact that quick-minded Aquarius likes to make decisions. Possibility one of the few problems may be a misunderstanding because an Aquarius mate is unpredictable at times, and for no reason at all, may seek seclusion and refuse to communicate. In that event, the best thing to do would be to let them enjoy their solitude. Both of these signs are naturally friendly people, while Libra is best at relationship. There may not be monumental disagreements between these two but Libra will need to understand the Aquarian perfectly.

LIBRA WITH PISCES

Libra is an air sign while Pisces is a water sign. This is a reasonably good combination. There is mutual attraction. This is especially true under intimate circumstances. Pisces will be content with Libra's exclusive company. They start off fine, since both are sentimental and affectionate. Pisces feels neglected, and whines and scolds. Pisces senses that Libra's commitment is often insincere and that Libra's charm is mostly superficial. But Libra's love of social affairs may generate jealousy and disharmony in the intimate life.

Libra can get along will with nice people, but the Pisces is more discriminating, and this is the source of their disagreements. There is a mutual appreciation for art and beauty and all that it entails between these two.

SCORPIO WITH OTHER ZODIAC SIGNS

SCORPIO WITH ARIES

Whereas Scorpio being a water sign and Aries being a fire sign. With Mars dominating both signs it makes for very positive temperaments unless there are some bad natal planetary aspects. Since Aries won't take orders from Scorpions and Scorpio will never take a back seat. Love cannot be a bonfire between these two. Though they've physical, energetic, and passionate in their sexual nature and each has a forceful personality and wants to control the other there is no room for these two. This combination is can make an ideal match if one ignores to dominate the other.

SCORPIO WITH TAURUS

These two are opposites in the zodiac, but they have more in common than other opposites. Both are determined and ambitious, and neither is much of a lover. These are zodiac opposites, but they are compatible earth and water signs. This usually manifests itself in a strong physical attraction. This combination mutually admires each other.

Jealousy however is the big problem with this pair and that seems to be always showing its face. Taurus must be careful to keep faith with the scorpion, or else this combination will fall down without warning.

SCORPIO WITH GEMINI

An air sign with a water sign. These two will have some difficulty rectifying their innate natures. Gemini is too changeable and inconstant for intense Scorpio, who needs and demands total commitment. Scorpio is basically a loner; Gemini likes to glitter in social settings. Gemini has a strong penchant for independence, while Scorpio wants to dominate and possess. Gemini's desire for freedom of action will clash with the jealous and possessive nature of Scorpio. These two will have some difficulty rectifying their innate natures. Then again, too much, stifles some. These two are opposites in the zodiac and are attracted to each other like magnets.

SCORPIO WITH CANCER

Both are ruled by water signs. Cancer is loyal; Scorpio's jealousy isn't provoked. Cancer admires Scorpio's strength while Scorpio finds a haven in Cancer's emotional commitment. Both are extremely intuitive and sense what will please the other. Together they can build a happy home where they feel safe and loved. This relationship has great intimacy, intensity, and depth. Things just get better all the time. Scorpio should make a good mate for quiet spoken cancer. Scorpio and cancer could well prove the ideal marriage combination.

SCORPIO WITH LEO

Leo being a fire sign and Scorpio being water sign. Two very strong willed individuals generally create some rather stormy moments. But Leo finds it hard to cope with Scorpio's jealousy and possessiveness. Scorpio considers Leo a showpiece. Scorpio doesn't understand Leo's need to be continually surrounded by an admiring audience. Scorpio would rather dominate than admire, and that doesn't suit Leo's kingly state. Two shinning personalities join together.

Basically this should make for one of the most compatible combinations, but long and happy partnership will be far better a Leo female marries a Scorpio male.

SCORPIO WITH VIRGO

Virgo belongs to the earth sign while Scorpio belongs to the water sign. The combination sometimes belongs to the mutual admiration society. If Virgo will keep from hurting Scorpio's pride, this combination will be happy and enduring. Scorpio is also possessive and fiercely loyal, which makes Virgo feel loved and protected. They also admire each other's minds. Virgo is logical, intellectual, and analytical. Scorpio is imaginative, visionary, and perceptive. Scorpio is volatile but secretive, Virgo is self-restrained and reserved. The Virgo mind is very fascinated with the mysterious and intriguing Scorpio. The only problem here is on the emotional side. If each of them keeps their emotion aside there is some hope for a longer lasting friendship.

SCORPIO WITH LIBRA

Libra is an air sign where as Scorpio is a water sign. Libra may find Scorpio's intense nature a bit overwhelming. Common goals and shared interests could avert any difficulties. There is much sympathetic magnetism between these two signs. While Scorpio is the more dominating sign of the two. There is much to recommend this union, for they have many sympathies in common. Librans are sentimental and susceptible as lovers. This seems to be appealing to Scorpio's dominant and possessive urges. As long as Libra does not hurt Scorpio's pride, Libran will find what they are looking for when they marry a Scorpio. Scorpio is also touchy, moody, and quick to lash out in anger, which is just the kind of person Libra cannot bear. Scorpio seethes and becomes steadily more jealous and demanding, Libra has either to submit-or to leave.

SCORPIO WITH SCORPIO

Since both belong to the water signs. These two people who are so much alike understand each other very little. They are highly jealous and demanding. Both are sulky, brooding, and possessive. Both are in a continual struggle to force the other to relinquish control. Where is a combination that is confusing in its outcome? If both individuals have a thorough understanding of their inherent traits, they can have deep sympathy for each other.

The dominant, possessive, and jealous temperaments of each are things which both will have to handle with extreme consideration. This can be a very good combination or a very bad one.

SCORPIO WITH SAGITTARIUS

Scorpio is a water sign and Sagittarius is a fire. The combination of these to signs is an affair without proper and secured future. Scorpio is dominant by nature, but Scorpio will have trouble keeping their Sagittarian partner under control. Sagittarius is open, talkative, and casual about relationships. Scorpio wants Sagittarius at home, Sagittarius wants to roam. Mutual distrust is easy here. The Scorpion possessiveness will make life unbearable for Sagittarius. Scorpio is attractive to the Sagittarian lust, but that is where the compatibility ends. Not a recommended combination. Live and learn is about the best thing to expect here. Both can bring out some of the other's better qualities but the chance of anything long lasting is remote.

SCORPIO WITH CAPRICORN

Scorpio belongs to a water sign and Capricorn is of earth sign. This is a very hard combination to analyse. Capricorn even likes Scorpio's jealousy-for that makes Capricorn feel secure. These two share a sense of purpose: they are ambitious, determined, and serious about responsibility-and as a team have good auguries for financial success. The emotional incompatibility usually becomes unbearable for the combination to handle. For practical matters there are common traits, but the stubborn nature of both signs could make them enemies when things get down and dirty.

SCORPIO WITH AQUARIUS

Scorpio being water sign and Aquarius being an air sign. The comparability often leads to a breaking affair. This combination usually ends up getting into unpleasant terms after a little time. Unpredictable Aquarius is too much for the solid Scorpio temperament. Aquarius has many of outside interests and this does not sit well with Scorpio. Aquarius is too reserved for the passionate Scorpio. Humanitarian instincts are what Scorpio admires in an Aquarian, but Scorpio has no interest in sharing them with the world.

Scorpio wants to possess the person and Aquarius want to own the world. Without some extremely mature attitude adjustment it will be difficult to rectify the inherent differences in each other's nature. Scorpio wants to stay at home; Aquarius wants to be free to go.

SCORPIO WITH PISCES

Everything seems fine until Pisces gets tired of the little interests that seem to keep Scorpio occupied outside of the home. Scorpio does not appreciate positive qualities of Pisces. Pisces' imagination sparks Scorpio's creativity. Pisces' intuitive awareness and Scorpio's depth of feeling unite in a special closeness. This kind of mating lasts. This may be a love at first sight combination, however it seldom lasts a long period of time. But, on the positive side there is an intuitive bond here that both will find agreeable. There is attraction and emotion and feelings and all that good stuff that they both like.

SAGITTARIUS WITH OTHER ZODIAC SIGNS

SAGITTARIUS WITH ARIES

The Mars-Jupiter duo is usually an ideal match for each other. Sagittarius is a perfect ideal and temperamental match for Aries. They both are active, spontaneous people. There may be a little conflict because both are impulsive and brutally frank. However, they have wonderful senses of humour and enjoy each other's company. If they make it in the bedroom, they'll make it everywhere else. Most people of these matches are in it for life. The Sagittarius means liberty, and the pursuit of happiness while Aries is subscribes to this theory. And for this reason, that makes them a good match.

SAGITTARIUS WITH TAURUS

These are two very different personality types the more reserved Taurus and the outgoing Sagittarius both has an appreciation for the truth. Sagittarius has an easy live and let live attitude this might work if Taurus can tie a string to Sagittarius's. The Taurus who marries a Sagittarian will find that no amount of arguing or berating is going to change the reckless Sagittarian With some understanding they can find harmony in their characters as long as they allow each other their personalities. With the Taurean being possessive and the Sagittarian being freedom loving, the Sagittarian may find this hard to co-operate with.

SAGITTARIUS WITH GEMINI

Mercury rules Gemini and Sagittarius are ruled by Jupiter the planet of knowledge and wisdom. Both have bright minds, but Sagittarius is outspoken while Gemini likes to enjoy fun. They are usually a compatible combination with both being frank, outspoken, and a certain amount of personal understanding being made. They meet on a common ground, and can plan their lives with equilibrium. They are restless, adventuresome, imaginative, and fun loving. No other opposite signs in the zodiac enjoy each other more than these two. However if Sagittarius forgoes its ego and Gemini restores to concrete planning they can make a good combination otherwise their combination may not last long.

SAGITTARIUS WITH CANCER

A water and fire combination. Sagittarius likes to wander, while Cancer is a prefers to stay at home. Cancer's commitment to total togetherness only makes Sagittarius desperate to get away. In addition, outspoken Sagittarius's bluntness continually wounds sensitive Cancer. They happen to be better friends than lovers. There is a vast difference in natures and the likely hood of being compatible is all but impossible, unless there are some positive aspects in their charts. Cancer is too needy for Sagittarius. On the good side, they are both generous people.

SAGITTARIUS WITH LEO

Both being of fire sign. The pendulum can swing in any body's favour. Together they share a liking for freedom, adventure, and meeting new people. Leo's natural quality of leadership brings out what loyalty Sagittarius can give. Leo is very proud, but self-confident and expansive Sagittarius is quite happy to let Leo go. Both love change and excitement and have a great zest for life. This is an excellent combination for the most part unless Sagittarius is in need of too much freedom and Leo becomes too bossy.

SAGITTARIUS WITH VIRGO

Virgo is an earth sign and Sagittarius is a fire sign. Their comparability often leads to unwanted and undesired conflicts. Though both are intellectual signs but the way their minds work clashes with each other. Sagittarius is expansive and extravagant, while Virgo prefers a simple, ordered, and unpretentious life. Sagittarius's free spirit has nothing in common with hardworking Virgo. The differences here are like day and night. Not all bad but difficult to reconcile with.

SAGITTARIUS WITH LIBRA

Libra being an air signs while Sagittarius being a fire sign. Their comparability is often marked by ego problems if one is able to forgo his/her ego this match can become a lasting affair. They will do well together, if Sagittarius can manage to be around enough to fulfil Libra's need for togetherness. Libra is stimulated by Sagittarius's eagerness for adventure, and Sagittarius is drawn to Libra's affectionate charm.

Both are highly romantic, though this quality is more dominant in Libra. Libra will want to settle down before flighty Sagittarius does, but they can work that out.

Charming, clever Libra knows how to appeal to Sagittarius's intellectual side and easily keeps Sagittarius intrigued. Sagittarius hates bondage and cannot be confined, and will not tolerate bondage, whether it be legal or not, and will use all the means at his command to break through bonds.

COMPATABILITY OF ZODIAC SIGNS

SAGITTARIUS WITH SCORPIO

Scorpio is a water sign and Sagittarius is a fire. The combination of these to signs is an affair without proper and secured future. Scorpio is dominant by nature, but Scorpio will have trouble keeping their Sagittarian partner under control. Sagittarius is open, talkative, and casual about relationships. Scorpio wants Sagittarius at home, Sagittarius wants to roam. Mutual distrust is easy here. The Scorpion possessiveness will make life unbearable for Sagittarius. Scorpio is attractive to the Sagittarian lust, but that is where the compatibility ends. Not a recommended combination. Live and learn is about the best thing to expect here. Both can bring out some of the other's better qualities but the chance of anything long lasting is remote.

SAGITTARIUS WITH SAGITTARIUS

Since both belong to fire signs. Their combination would be a sweet- sour affair. Two lively, optimistic people on the go all the time. But this exciting, chaotic, eventful relationship is too unpredictable to suit either of them. They have a tendency to bring out the worst in each other. Each remains uncommitted and has so many outside interests that this pair inevitably drifts apart. If this combination is not on the same intellectual and social plane, there is little hope for this couple to have a long happy relationship. They will have to do everything together or nothing at all. All interests being social and business must be the same. May work better as friends or partners.

SAGITTARIUS WITH CAPRICORN

Sagittarius belongs to a fire sign whereas Capricorn attributes to earth sign. Sagittarius is venturesome, sociable, and expansive.

Capricorn is cautious with money and concerned with appearances and Sagittarius is neither. Both should look elsewhere. Capricorn and the outgoing, risk taking Sagittarius. Not much in the way of compatibility but as with most combinations they can learn from each other. Sagittarius may prove to be too much for the sombre and restrictive temperament of Capricorn. Their temperament is entirely different, one is optimistic, and the other is pessimistic. Here again we see the difference between them may not be a lasting affair.

SAGITTARIUS WITH AQUARIUS

Sagittarius is a fire sign whereas Aquarius is an air sign. Their comparability often results in a powerful combination. Each of the other has to forgo his or her own ego. Aquarius is innovative. Sagittarius loves to experiment. These two share a great zest for living and a forward-looking viewpoint. Neither will try to tie down the other. Both seek to explore possibilities to the fullest, and they share idealism about love and life. They'll like each other too. The combination usually has a great chance for success. Both temperaments are very much alike. This is a purely social combination that will revel in a large group of friends and public-spirited associates. Sagittarius readily understands the moods and peculiarities of the Aquarius. There is a very good chance for a successful relationship.

SAGITTARIUS WITH PISCES

Sagittarius is a fire sign and Pisces is water. There is much here for an interesting and sincere relationship. Sagittarius is attracted to Pisces's spirituality. Sagittarius being free and easy will find Pisces too much of a heavy load to haul around. Though, Sagittarius may find that the marriage to Pisces is too confining. There will be a lot of confusion and wonder between these two. At times it will be good and at other times not good at all. Your natures are somewhat opposite to one another and the ability to understand the other's intent and actions will be evident. This combination quite hard to match.

CAPRICORN WITH OTHER ZODIAC SIGNS

CAPRICORN WITH ARIES

Capricorns are usually patient and are traditionally easygoing. Arians are too impatient to cope with the slowness attitude. Saturn represents the Capricorn and Mars governs the Aries. Aries's taste for innovation and experiment may not please Capricorns. Aries is restless, fiery, and impulsive; Capricorn is ordered, settled, and practical. Capricorn needs to dominate and so does Aries. Problems often crops up over moneymaking schemes. Not a hopeful combination. Capricorn will nod against the Arian will and a disagreement is bound to occur. In the matter of sex there is an affinity; however, their inherent personalities clash. The combination of a fire sign with an earth sign. Aries is a fiery in nature while Capricorn is earth, cautious and reserved. Aries prefers to take action while Capricorn would rather plan and wait. Without a great deal of tolerance and patience, there is not much hope for this union.

CAPRICORN WITH TAURUS

A good combination of the basic earth signs. Both are responsible and practical natures. They even have a mutual desire for success and material things. Capricorn is a strong match for Taurus, for they both have passions that are straightforward and uncomplicated. Capricorn is a bit more secretive than Taurus.

With both partners having mutual understanding of each other's personalities this can be a very compatible marriage. Venus and Saturn blend very well from an emotional point of view.

CAPRICORN WITH GEMINI

Capricorn gets worried about security, while Gemini feels about losing its liberty. The Saturn ruled Capricorn will be at differences with the Mercury ruled Gemini. Patience is a virtue with Capricorn, but it is not so with Gemini. Gemini's need for a survival does nothing to make Capricorn feel secure. Gemini's free talks, meets opposition from conservative Capricorn. Capricorn's great drive to execute will prove to be too much for the Gemini. Until they both are ready to minimize their goals. Capricorn will go on hunting until he gains the upper hand. Of course with these two people going together anything is possible and the outcome of the result may not be satisfying to each other.

CAPRICORN WITH CANCER

Both signs have plenty in common. Capricorn has too many other interests to give Cancer all the attention it needs. Cancer is shy, sensitive, and needs affection, while Capricorn is aloof, and domineering. Capricorn has the ability to make cancer's dream come true, while Cancer is happy wishing for and wanting the success and security that the Capricorn strives for. The elements of water and earth go well together but these are zodiac opposites you can expect both side of the coin. They will have to take the good with the bad and there will be plenty of both. Capricorn lacks the warmth and sentiment that Cancer requires.

CAPRICORN WITH LEO

Leo being a fire signs whereas Capricorn is an earth sign. The combination of these two may at time lead to severe complications. The slow Capricorn may prove to be too much for the carefree nature of Leo. Leo will think Capricorn stingy with affection because Capricorn's reserved, undemonstrative nature cannot give Leo the adoration it needs. Neither will take a back seat nor let the other dominate.

This affair will be on the rocks before it even leaves the dock. Leo forgives and forgets; Capricorn being the one who is slow to anger and seldom forgets. This pair would not form the ideal basis for mutual understanding. Leo likes to live for the moment and Capricorn prefers to make calculated movements.

CAPRICORN WITH VIRGO

Since these are two earth signs the mercury and sun combination should find mutual grounds for an agreeable partnership. A harmonious pair. Both are diligent, disciplined, and have a sense of purpose. They admire one another and take great pride in pleasing each other. Both need respect and approval and each intuitively gives the other exactly that. With these two signs there are some similarity and compatibility. They are both very exacting. This stops many areas of disagreement. They both take great pride in appearance and surroundings.

CAPRICORN WITH LIBRA

Libra is an air sign whereas Capricorn is an earth sign. Capricorn believes in hard work and achievement at any price. Libra is fond of socializing and nightlife, while Capricorn tends to be a loner, comfortable with only a chosen few.

Libra needs flattery and attention, but Capricorn keeps its affections buried. Capricorn. And Libra's lazy, easygoing ways will offend. On the surface these two seem to be on the opposite, but the Capricorn is very much influenced by Libra. If Libra does not find the steady Capricorn nature too boring, there is good chance here for a successful marriage. Libra had better screen the social environment to suit Capricorn's views or there may be some embarrassing moments later on. Unless Capricorn can open up a little more there could be problems here. Libra requires affection and Capricorn tends to put it off.

CAPRICORN WITH SCORPIO

Scorpio belongs to a water sign and Capricorn is of earth sign. This is a very hard combination to analyse. Capricorn even likes Scorpio's jealousy-for that makes Capricorn feel secure. These two share a sense of purpose: they are ambitious, determined, and serious about responsibility-and as a team have good auguries for financial success.

The emotional incompatibility usually becomes unbearable for the combination to handle. For practical matters there are common traits, but the stubborn nature of both signs could make them enemies when things get down and dirty.

CAPRICORN WITH SAGITTARIUS

Sagittarius belongs to a fire sign whereas Capricorn attributes to earth sign. Sagittarius is venturesome, sociable, and expansive. Capricorn is cautious with money and concerned with appearances and Sagittarius is neither. Both should look elsewhere. Capricorn and the outgoing, risk taking Sagittarius. Not much in the way of compatibility but as with most combinations they can learn from each other. Sagittarius may prove to be too much for the sombre and restrictive temperament of Capricorn. Their temperament is entirely different, one is optimistic, and the other is pessimistic. Here again we see the difference between them may not be a lasting affair.

CAPRICORN WITH CAPRICORN

Both belong to earth sign. They both have the same faults, which may keep fault finding down to a minimum. With important issues, they would both have what it takes to over come any hardship. Capricorns approve of people like themselves, so with these two there's no lack of mutual respect and regard. Neither one can relax or let down its hair. Both have the same long-range aspirations and the basic qualities to attain them. Great mixture for a happy relationship. The biggest problem here will be keeping things lively and new.

CAPRICORN WITH AQUARIUS

Since Capricorn being an earth sign and Aquarius being an air sign Capricorn believes in self-discipline and Aquarius believes in self-expression. Capricorn finds Aquarius too unpredictable, and Aquarius's impersonal attitude makes Capricorn uneasy. However, they should like each other and love can turn into friendship. This is a very hard combination to analyse. Capricorn wants all effort and anything else Aquarius has to give- to be cantered at home for their mutual good.

Capricorn does not like the interest that Aquarius shows to other people. A very doubtful combination.

Too many other differences as well and unless you have other compatible aspects in your birth charts, don't expect a long lasting affair.

CAPRICORN WITH PISCES

As Capricorn being an earth sign and Pisces being a water sign. This is a good combination with complimentary values. And there's nothing Capricorn likes better than being admired. Pisces generous affections and Capricorn's strong sense of loyalty combine to make each feel safe and protected. These very different people meet each other's needs. One of the things that Pisces will admire about Capricorn is his very practical ways. This combination seems to work very well, provided each other admires the other's values first.

AQUARIUS WITH OTHER ZODIAC SIGNS

Aquarius belongs to an air sign whereas Aries belongs to fire sign. Both signs are of independent nature but at times Aquarius will do things without notice with which Aries may become impatient. Since both are active, ambitious, enjoy a wide range of interests, and are equally eager for sexual adventure. As both are independent Aquarius energies more than Aries and Aries may at times feel neglected. Aries finds the Aquarian unpredictability exciting, but feels entirely insecure. However, with a bit of tact and understanding on both sides, this is a great affair that could turn into something even better. This could possibly be a good relationship, but will require a positive attitude on both parts.

AQUARIUS WITH TAURUS

These two live on opposite sides of the planet, in fact some times, Taurus will wonder if Aquarius is even from this planet. Neither is likely to approve of the other. Taurus is conservative, careful, closemouthed. Aquarius is unconventional, innovative, and vivacious. Taurus is lusty and passionate while Taurus needs security and comfort. Aquarius, a fancy-free loner who resents ties that bind. This combination heads in for many difficulties. The Aquarian being unpredictable. Both love ease and comfort but their views on how to obtain them are very different. Another big irritation for the Taurus lover is the unwillingness of the Aquarius to share his secrets.

Aquarius will find the Taurus attention somewhat smothering and restrictive

AQUARIUS WITH GEMINI

Gemini is bit inconstant or unstable, Aquarius understands somewhat Gemini's needs. Gemini is always looking for surprises and the Aquarian can give them. Gemini and Aquarius get along quite easily. They share a taste for new things, travelling, meeting new people and doing new things. Since both are unpredictable, things may always go smoothly with them. But love keeps getting them together, for Aquarius adores Gemini's wit and good cheer. The caring, thoughts of Aquarius will find a smooth home with Gemini. Uranus, the ruling planet of Aquarius, is full of surprises and sudden changes. This will suit the Gemini perfectly.

There will be plenty of none stop variety to afford the stimulation that Gemini needs for its dual personality and goal.

AQUARIUS WITH CANCER

Aquarius is quick-minded, unpredictable, and apt to be impatient with cautious, hesitant Cancer. Cancer has a conservative taste while Aquarius taste is usually the opposite. Cancer needs to feel close and secure. The social side of the Aquarian may prove to be too much for the Cancer. Aquarian's love to share their life stories with the world while cancer is satisfied to concentrate on personal obligations. Odds against this combination are too great for this combination, unless one will become convergent to the other. Aquarius has a need to be independent and often appears detached in a close relationship with cancer.

AQUARIUS WITH LEO

Aquarius is an air sign and Leo is a fire sign. The comparability of this two in terms of worldly affairs can often become difficult to match. Both like socializing and meeting new people, but Leo always needs to perform on center stage, which makes Aquarius impatient and irritable. Aquarius is too independent to become Leo's devoted subject. And that's where it ends. Leo views Aquarius's aloof emotions as a personal rejection. Both signs are better when doing things for others. Leo loves the world and Aquarius loves humanity. This makes for an excellent combination for a partnership that deals with or caters to the public. Each has a mutual understanding of the other when it comes to intimate matters, needs and desires.

AQUARIUS WITH VIRGO

Aquarius is an air sign while Virgo is an earth sign. Aquarius has venturesome ideas and thinks Virgo unresponsive or cold. A lot depends on the cultural and educational levels of the partners. Aquarius is interested in other people, causes and Virgo is cautious about emotional giving. Virgo seeks personal achievement and financial security. Aquarius is outgoing, inventive, a visionary. Virgo is reserved, prudent, and very practical about its ambitions. This couple may not even make it as friends. There is a marked difference between the two; the chances for a happy and enduring marriage are almost nil.

Each has a distant quality. There is no happy medium with this combination; it is either very good or very bad.

AQUARIUS WITH LIBRA

Whereas both are air signs. They both have basically the same interests and qualities, so there would be great understanding in the relationship. The biggest problem may be unresolved conflicts, as neither wants to stir the pot when differences appear. Equally demonstrative, lively, warm, sociable, in love with beautiful things, a problem is that neither wants to face reality. Though they are charming, peace loving, and adaptable, each needs a stronger balance than the other can provide. Also, because they are so much alike. Here is a match made in heaven, unless one had an incompatible sign rising at birth.. While both likes to be admired. With this combination there is so much in common and so little negatives

AQUARIUS WITH SCORPIO

Aquarius being an air sign and Scorpio being water sign. The comparability often leads to a breaking affair. This combination usually ends up getting into unpleasant terms after a little time. Unpredictable Aquarius is too much for the solid Scorpio temperament. Aquarius has many of outside interests and this does not sit well with Scorpio. Aquarius is too reserved for the passionate Scorpio. Humanitarian instincts are what Scorpio admires in an Aquarian, but Scorpio has no interest in sharing them with the world. Scorpio wants to possess the person and Aquarius want to own the world. Without some extremely mature attitude adjustment it will be difficult to rectify the inherent differences in each other's nature. Scorpio wants to stay at home; Aquarius wants to be free to go.

AQUARIUS WITH SAGITTARIUS

Aquarius is an air sign where as Sagittarius is a fire sign. Their comparability often results in a powerful combination. Each of the other has to forgo his or her own ego. Aquarius is innovative. Sagittarius loves to experiment. These two share a great zest for living and a forward-looking viewpoint. Neither will try to tie down the other. Both seek to explore possibilities to the fullest, and they share idealism about love and life. They'll like each other too.

The combination usually has a great chance for success. Both temperaments are very much alike. This is a purely social combination that will revel in a large group of friends and public-spirited associates. Sagittarius readily understands the moods and peculiarities of the Aquarius. There is a very good chance for a successful relationship.

AQUARIWITH CAPRICORN

Aquarius being an air sign and Capricorn being an earth sign. Capricorn believes in self-discipline and Aquarius believes in self-expression. Capricorn finds Aquarius too unpredictable, and Aquarius's impersonal attitude makes Capricorn uneasy. However, they should like each other and love can turn into friendship. This is a very hard combination to analyse. Capricorn wants all effort and anything else Aquarius has to give- to be cantered at home for their mutual good. Capricorn does not like the interest that Aquarius shows to other people. A very doubtful combination. Too many other differences as well and unless you have other compatible aspects in your birth charts, don't expect a long lasting affair.

AQUARIUS WITH AQUARIUS

Both being an air signs. This combination is more compatible then any other combination. One Aquarius finally finds just the right mate in the other Aquarian. They admire and like each other, and especially enjoy each other's sense of humor. Each is involved in all kinds of projects and friendships. With so many outside activities going, they are likely to be apart as much as they are together and that's fine with them. They haven't a thing to quarrel about since they agree on everything: Both of them are much more rational than emotional.

AQUARIUS WITH PISCES

Aquarius is an air sign where as Pisces is a water sign. Their comparability often leads to an unconventional relationship. Pisces needs someone strong to take control. Aquarius shuns any kind of emotional demands. This can be a dreamy affair as someone should show the reality to these people and that's not to say that they are unaware of reality. Both operate in a different manner than the other signs.

If the Pisces is able give the Aquarius the benefit of the doubt, the marriage should be a lasting one.

PISCES WITH OTHER ZODIAC SIGNS

PISCES WITH ARIES

Pisceans are romantic and they desire the delicate approach that which the Arian lacks. Aries will draw Pisces out of their shell, and in turn will be appealed by Pisces mysterious nature in terms of sexuality. The boldness and confidence of Aries adding to the Pisces's intuitions and fantasies end in an eventful union. Pisces is somewhat shy and Aries likes to be dominant, Pisces likes having someone to be looked upon. For a happy coupling thus requires only a little more tact on Arian part.

PISCES WITH TAURUS

These two can share a great deal of their appreciation for beauty, art, and sensuality and just about any of the finer things in life. Pisces may not altogether understand Taurus's materialistic approach to life.

Taurus's practical, easygoing nature helps Pisces through its frequent changes of mood. In love, Taurus is devoted and Pisces adores. This usually is a very happy combination. Pisces being romantic, imaginative, impressionable and flexible is just what the Taurus native is looking for.

PISCES WITH GEMINI

Their passion is quite high, and so are their problems. Thoughtless Gemini easily hurts Pisces. Gemini is mischievous and playful, but Pisces is sensitive and takes things to heart easily. Each practices in his or her thoughts in their own way: Gemini needs freedom and Pisces needs unending appreciation. Pisces just can't feel secure with talkative moods of Gemini, and he tries to pull the net in his own way. This atmosphere eventually makes it hard for Gemini to breathe his own liberty. The freedom of Gemini is stake if he marries a Piscean. Gemini's should be prepared to change their ways if they want to seek happiness with a loving and possessive Piscean.

PISCES WITH CANCER

The water signs rule a harmonious match and quite a perfect match as both. The sentimental combination of these two signs makes for an ideal marriage. Although both will have their moments of gloom and doom, they will soon come out in the sunshine to forgive and forget each other. They are both romantic, need to love and be loved and can probably communicate to each other without speaking or making facial gestures. Both are emotional, intensely devoted, and sensitive to each other's moods.

PISCES WITH LEO

A fire and water combination. Leo being a fire sign and Pisces being a water sign often makes this a unique combination. Both are more inclined to take than to give. Fiery Leo and watery Pisces.

This is the depiction of these two. Generally not expected to work but both have an ability to learn from one another if they can get past their innate differences. The strong and hearty temperament of Leo may be too much for the subtle and sensitive Pisces. Pisces, with resilience, takes on the changing moods of any partnership. While Leo is flattered by the dependency of others. Pisces may be too much for Leo to take over a long period of time.

PISCES WITH VIRGO

Pisces is fascinated by Virgo's incisive, analytical mind. Virgo, love means security and mental compatibility. Pisces is the very opposite of Virgo as opposites often are sentimental and are poles apart. It will take a great deal of patience and understanding on the part of Virgo to cope with the sentimental nature of Pisces. This is another pair of zodiac opposites that can be great at times and horrible at others times. The opposites can learn a lot about themselves from their counterparts. It will go a long way in making this combination happy

PISCES WITH LIBRA

Libra is an air sign while Pisces is a water sign. This is a reasonably good combination. There is mutual attraction. This is especially true under intimate circumstances. Pisces will be content with Libra's exclusive company. They start off fine, since both are sentimental and affectionate. Pisces feels neglected, and whines and scolds. Pisces senses that Libra's commitment is often insincere and that Libra's charm is mostly superficial. But Libra's love of social affairs may generate jealousy and disharmony in the intimate life. Libra can get along will with nice people, but the Pisces is more discriminating, and this is the source of their disagreements. There is a mutual appreciation for art and beauty and all that it entails between these two.

PISCES WITH SCORPIO

Everything seems fine until Pisces gets tired of the little interests that seem to keep Scorpio occupied outside of the home. Scorpio does not appreciate positive qualities of Pisces. Pisces' imagination sparks Scorpio's creativity.

Pisces' intuitive awareness and Scorpio's depth of feeling unite in a special closeness. This kind of mating lasts. This may be a love at first sight combination, however it seldom lasts a long period of time. But, on the positive side there is an intuitive bond here that both will find agreeable. There is attraction and emotion and feelings and all that good stuff that they both like.

PISCES WITH SAGITTARIUS

Sagittarius is a fire sign and Pisces is a water Sign. There is much here for an interesting and sincere relationship. Sagittarius is attracted to Pisces's spirituality. Sagittarius being free and easy will find Pisces too much of a heavy load to haul around. Though Sagittarius may find that the marriage to Pisces is too confining. There will be a lot of confusion and wonder between these two. At times it will be good and at other times not good at all. Your natures are somewhat opposite to one another and the ability to understand the other's intent and actions will be evident.

PISCES WITH CAPRICORN

As Capricorn being an earth sign and Pisces being Water sign. This is a good combination with complimentary values. And there's nothing Capricorn likes better than being admired. Pisces generous affections and Capricorn's strong sense of loyalty combine to make each feel safe and protected. These very different people meet each other's needs. One of the things that Pisces will admire about Capricorn is his very practical ways. This combination seems to work very well, provided each other admires the other's values first.

PISCES WITH AQUARIUS

Both being an Air Sign. This combination is more compatible then any other combination. One Aquarius finally finds just the right mate in the other Aquarian. They admire and like each other, and especially enjoy each other's sense of humour. Each is involved in all kinds of projects and friendships. With so many outside activities going, they are likely to be apart as much as they are together and that's fine with them. They haven't a thing to quarrel about since they agree on everything. Both of them are much more rational than emotional.

PISCES WITH PISCES

Since both belong to water sign, having the same virtues and vices they should get along well together, at least they will have understanding and sympathy for one another. They find it hard to cope with practical realities, and there's no strong partner around to push either one in the right direction. Both have the same interests and the same love of home and possessions. At least both can be anchored to each other, so that they can put their shoulders to the wheel and face the responsibilities that reality demands. They have the refinement and delicacy that each desires. This should be a good combination.

CHAPTER SEVENTEEN

NUMEROLOGY

Know About Your Self through Numerology
KNOW YOUR FUTURE THROUGH NUMBERS
IF YOU ARE BORN ON THE FOLLOWING DATE OF ANY
MONTH. YOUR FORECAST READS AS: YOUR RULING
NO.1 (ONE)
IF YOU BORN ON THE 1. (FIRST) 10th (TENTH), 19th
(NINETEENTH) OR 28th (TWENTY-EIGHTH) OF ANY
MONTH THAN KINDLY READ THE FOLLOWING:
THE NUMBER ONES

In general ones are leaders independent active, speedy, adventures, original and easily bored. One take a heroic stance in life and thrive on obstacles which they prefer to see as challenge They are depressed when they are not achieving their ideals (which are very strong and positive rarely unrealistic. Ones love what is new in the fashion scene. They pride themselves on being up to that and ahead in their thinking. They identify with groundbreakers pioneers achievers. They are dominant peoples with a great deal of fairs they are ambitious decisive and often have an ironic scene of humor.

IF YOU BORN ON THE 1. FIRST

You strive to stand in the first from the crowd. A natural leader you have a strong will and need to goal to work towards. You may run yours own business. You do not take no for an answer but have to push yourself to follow through (you tend to procrastinate). You like to plan rather than implement and are talented in diagnosis and troubleshooting. You are the one of the most idealistic people but consider yourself pragmatic rather than emotional. You may not be demonstrative emotionally but you love very deeply and are sometime romantic. You value loyalty very highly. You want things to be done correctly.

IF YOU BORN ON THE 10th

You have great deal of vitality and recover yourself from any setback. You are creative and have much interest and are always forward thinking. You may have little help from others because you structure situation so that you are I n dispensable you would do well in design.

IF YOU BORN ON THE 19th

Take note this is one of the four Karmic numbers and signifies that you have chosen some special direction or have a special goal in life you will always being trying to fulfil It; your nature is complex due to the combination of the one and the nine. Extremely discerning and perceptive you may put up an aloof or formal front use your intellect as a shield until you get to know someone. Verbal sparring and a keen sense of humour usually a dry wit characterize your social interaction your emotional attachment are deep but you strive to maintain self-control at all times your negative attribute is often cynicism, rigidly, or xenophobia.

IF YOU BORN ON THE 28th

You love your independence and freedom and yet are much more loving and affectionate than other ones. You love to be the center of attraction with people that you admire and respect. You always have quality friends. Your mate will have to be a strong person in his/her own right. And you will never settle for less then your ideal.

Like all ones you are an executive capable of sacrificing for your ambition, you would be successful in any profession, especially teaching, law engineering, architecture, and design. You have dramatic flair in you all do and will chosen a mate who shares this trait.

IF YOU BORN ON THE 2. (SECOND) OR 11th (ELEVENTH), OR 20th (TWENTIETH) OR 29th (TWENTY-NINTH) OF ANY MONTH THAN KINDLY READ THE FOLLOWING:
THE NUMBER TWOS

In general Twos are very sensitive emotional people. They do not have the one raging ambition but are content to work more in the back ground often as support for more dominant people. Two's analyses a situation and are conscious of the dynamics of emotional interrelationships at work and at home. They tend toward perfectionism (even-net picking) and should be allowed to work at their own pace. They will do anything to bring harmony into situation and often they will stay with an unpleasant situation longer then they should.

Two's tend to be plagued by worries that stem from a fear of the unknown.

IF YOU BORN ON THE 2. SECOND

Your social life and the mate are very important to your sense of well-being. You may find more accomplishment through having good friends then you do from your employment. You are easily affected from environment and should only work with people with whom you are compatible. In a conflict, you tend to be a peacemaker.

You may not let on what your real feelings are in the conflict. You may work long hours to please someone. You crave affection and usually remember other people's birthdays. You reply conversation looking for things you might say or wondering if someone has an ulterior motive. You are high strung and should not overtax your talents for music and arts. You love beautiful things but often don't want to push yourself to get them. You are patient and excel at detail work. Do not compare yourself and your accomplishment with those who may have more assertive or competitive numbers.

IF YOU BORN ON THE 11th

your birth date is the master of inspiration. All Twos are sensitive and this is especially true for you. This is the number of the teacher or of someone who function as exemplar. If you are female you may be unusually pretty. If male you may have refined characteristics or be interested in aesthetic pursuits. You may find yourself in the limelight. Successful areas are Television, poetry, metaphysics, art, psychology and spiritual work. You have a tendency to fall in love with peoples and ideas. You may always be on the verge of success yearning to do something almost impossible. Eleven can fall into menial work while nurturing a strong sense that they are meant for better things. Try to find some talent that you can express.

IF YOU BORN ON THE 20th

You are extremely conscientious person, friendly, compassionate, and eager to help. You may do well in small business but will probably not want to take on a large project without help from others. You will be attracted by spiritual matters and do quite a bit of searching through out your life.

You would make a sensitive therapist, artist, photographer, or writer on subject of interest of women. You work slowly because of attention to detail. You need to order to help you from feeling anxious.

IF YOU BORN ON THE 29th

Your spiritual interest is generally heightened. Your number adds up too eleven, which is the master number of inspiration in the mystical spiritual world. Like the 11, you need to stay grounded by activities that offer discipline and immediate reward (such as working in the garden, cooking, sewing, and building). You will have to watch your moods and know what to do before they get out of hand. You may be an inspiration to others and may attract the lime light through teaching or your art. You can also find success in occupations such as accounting and waiting tables, while pursuing your artistic interest. If a women, you may be very pretty, or as a man you have rather gentlemanly features.

IFYOU BORN ON THE 3. (THIRD) OR 12th (TWELFTH), OR 21st (TWENTY FIRST) OR 30th (THIRTIETH) OF ANY MONTH THAN KINDLY READ THE FOLLOWING:
THE NUMBER THREES

Happy outgoing, forever, optimistic, vivacious, talkative, scattered all these describe the threes. Lovers of social life and recreation, Threes do not enjoy hard physical employment. They may excel at sales and will always have several projects going on at once. Work must feel creative for them to be happy. They are not overly concern about money or the future. They are spontaneous and impulsive. They must learn to be focused and not overly self-indulge. When positive they bring joy and light to all situations. All Threes easily overcome physical illness.

IF YOU WERE BORN ON THE 3rd

You are charming quick to see the humor in any situation but can be somewhat unreliable. You may spread yourself thin over several projects because you like to keep busy. You are energetic, but easily distracted.

Your social life is of a great concern to you. Having many friends you need to budget a sizeable amount of gifts because you are also generous. You love spontaneous get-together and may be the one in the office to suggest the going out of drinks or taking up a collection for a birthday party. You naturally embellish stories and events. You are known for youthfulness, certain intensity in style and while friends may laugh about your scattered ness, you are love by them. You adore an audience. Creative hobbies are a necessity for you.

IF YOU WERE BORN ON THE 12th

You have one of the most magnetic birth dates. You have an exceptional ability to express yourself, be convincing, and persuade others.

Your mind goes right to the heart at any issue. You are idealistic, yet logical and can be brilliant. You are easily bored and often tired of people ones you have picked their brains. You have a great need to charm and need to flirt. Your eye for color and design, especially in photography, is outstanding. You love the media-movies, magazines, and television and keep up to date on who is who. You are something of a celebrity of yourself.

IF YOU WERE BORN ON THE 21st

You may be a bit quieter and less impulsive then other Threes, very sensitive and more likely to think things through before speaking. You have a great imagination and may be prone to dreaming, perhaps writing poetry. You may be natural singer or songwriter. You may be content to have fewer, but closer friends then other Threes. You are high strung and should avoid analyzing things too much. You may find you have a tendency of infatuations (due to seeing people in a rosier light through your imagination and sense of drama). You may be gullible. You love pleasure and aesthetic pursuits. You definitely avoid manual labour if at all possible.

IF YOU WERE BORN ON THE 30th

You have exceptional high energy. Your enthusiasm is infectious; you can motivate and persuade others. You are outspoken and have a flair for having just the right word or fact to win an argument. You may have strong psychic ability. You would be an excellent teacher, actor, or musician. You would make a wonderful insister. You are serious and intense about what interest you, but will find it difficult to fulfil old promises. Like other Threes, you are flirtatious. Guard against a tendency to drink too much or overspend on cloths and socializing.

IF YOU BORN ON THE 4. (FOURTH) OR 13th (THIRTEEN), OR 22nd (TWENTY SECOND) OR 31st (THIRTY FIRST) OF ANY MONTH THAN KINDLY READ THE FOLLOWING: THE NUMBER FOURS

In general those with a birth date of four are called the "salt of the earth". Loyal, productive, earnest, Fours love home, family, and country. They prefer secure environments and stability. They take a cautious approach and enjoy working with their hands. They are builders and managers. While Fours are traditionalist they are also enthusiastic supporters of measure that result in reform, improvement and efficiency.

IF YOU WERE BORN ON THE 4th

You succeed through business, management, production, and anything connected to building and the earth. You learn things the hard way and have confidence that you can learn anything if shown the principles. You may have trouble seeing the "big picture". You can be very cautious and careful in approach to work and life in general.

You must make an effort to keep up to date. With fundamentals no frill thinking you have strong ideas about the right way to do things. You may work on several manual jobs in your life before working your way up to a position where your experience is respected.

IF YOU WERE BORN ON THE 13th

You do well in business involved with manufacturing commerce real estate and building (especially remodeling). You are more capable of verbal expression then those born on the 4th and posses creative ability that absorb you. You would like to be more socially successful, find a great deal of satisfaction in your work. You have an exceptional ability to reform and improve any situation or condition. You may have strong emotional nature that erupts suddenly because you have tendency to ignore your feelings.

IF YOU WERE BORN ON THE 22nd

This minister number requires you to work for the universal good rather then for personal ambition. This means that spiritual study should be a large part of your education. You are competent at almost anything you undertake. You will find that your varied experiences will someday be appropriate in a very challenging project. Your work must meet your ideals; you may pursue a hobby because you feel it will eventually pay off. You are not interested in status or luxury, but in making a significant contribution and living your life in a meaningful manner. You may have many Aquarian friends. You will recognize a special quality in others Twenty-two you meet, who will also display originality, competence and reformative abilities. You can be single minded and serious and need to feel in control. You must realize your power is channeled from above. You are sensitive, analytic, and judgmental.

IF YOU WERE BORN ON THE 31st

You derive great satisfaction from working with your hands and may be a sculptor or painter. You may have very high ambition for yourself. You are very traditional love your friends and remember their birthdays. You may be a great cook. You love to travel and socialize, but work for extremely long hours if motivated. You do not enjoy living alone and will take on solicitous attitude towards your mate. You love talk about yourself and your plans and expected others to be interested.

IF YOU BORN ON THE 5 (FIFTH) OR 14th (FOURTEENTH), OR 23rd (TWENTY THIRD) OF ANY MONTH THAN KINDLY READ THE FOLLOWING:
THE NUMBER FIVES

In general, Fives are active, adaptable, curious people who insist on your independence. They prefer flexible hours and will always add a new dimension to what ever they do. Fives are very good sales people gregarious and persuasive. Fives love a good deal and want to be successful. They are spontaneous and know how to take advantage of an opportunity. They move quickly and do not brood over losses.

They are charming not always too serious and love being the devil's advocate. Fives open new territory, promote big business deals, and do not except the word "can't".

IF YOU WERE BORN ON THE 5th

You enjoy travelling. You may want to marry late so that you can explore first. Adventures, you need work that is challenging, risky, and different. You would be an excellent promoter being something of a ham yourself. You are known as a good storyteller and jokester and will learn much through love affairs. You tend to use things up quickly and seek new stimulation. You are always on the alert, curious, and questioning and love to rock the boat. You will have a variety of jobs and will leave home early to seek your fortune, which, you are convinced in just around the corner. You see yourself as something of a hobo prince or lucky lady.

IF YOU WERE BORN ON THE 14th

You may have most interesting life, studded with setbacks that cannot keep you down. You must be careful to know your boundaries. You will meet people throughout your life with which you feel a "karmic" connection. You are vigorous, competitive and can be discipline when there is some short-term goal to be gained. You like to experiment and crave stimulation. You should be in business for yourself; anything to do wit travel, promotion, the public, performing and

Entertainment appeals to you. You want to live, not just exist. You may have a very opinionated nature based on what you have "experienced in the past". You have a highly visible sexual nature. You may be eccentric.

IF YOU WERE BORN ON THE 23rd

You are extremely independence and self-sufficient. You may have an eccentricity for which you are known. You may be interested in art and music or new age ideals. You have an interesting way of viewing life and turns events to your advantage. Verbal expression, witty, and, at times, defiant you can be petty and critical under stress. Generally however you excel in persuasion and know what other peoples will buy. You may appear youthful a long time.

IF YOU BORN ON THE 6 (SIXTH) OR 15th (FOURTEENTH), OR 24th (TWENTY FOURTH) OF ANY MONTH THAN KINDLY READ THE FOLLOWING:
THE NUMBER SIXES

In general, those with a Six birth dates are the responsible type who prefer traditional lifestyle and domestic comfort. They are parents, teachers, practical artist, and healers. They accomplish through their hands and hearts. Sixes are often plagued by worries, and will wither if not doing something useful. Great community workers and upholders of moral justice, they understand compromise, and always search for an answer that serves the broadest interest. They are stubborn in their opinion as to what is "right".

IF YOU WERE BORN ON THE 6th

You have a very loving, but territorial nature. You are natural teacher and your ideas on how to parent are strong. Your home is of the uttermost importance to you; you take responsibilities very seriously. You love luxuries and crave romantic attention. You may have necessary worries about "going broke", something which seldom happens to Sixes since you are able to find financial backing for your business ideas. Your social position and contacts are important to you. You know the value of reciprocity. Family and friends always come first. Buy a good backpack and/or well- outfitted camper.

IF YOU WERE BORN ON THE 15th

Your home is very important to you. You have great financial protection (all Sixes do), and people come to you for advice. You are more open-minded, spirited, independent, and well-travelled then other Sixes. If female, you need a carrier outside the home (although you consider your home an accomplishment in itself). You would make great fashion or interior designer, emergency nurse, or teacher. You need a wide social circle of educated people as friends. Your family is your first priority, but friends soon become "family" to you. You can be quite creative. Singing is a possible talent; at the very least, you will be noted for a pleasing voice.

IF YOU WERE BORN ON THE 24th

You want to build a family empire. You will be very unhappy alone or without domestic responsibilities. You love to accumulate wealth for yourself and others and will do well in traditional occupation such as teaching, accounting, banking, and real estate. Your ideas were set earlier in life and will tend not to change. Your admire creative and spontaneous people and may be inclined to marry one (since you feel very secure with your own abilities). You consider yourself liberal and open; other may not. You may be very emotional or prone to jealousy. You are careful, cautious and productive. Most of your plans come to fruition.

IF YOU BORN ON THE 7 (SEVENTH) OR 16th (SIXTEENTH), OR 25th (TWENTY FIFTH) OF ANY MONTH THAN KINDLY READ THE FOLLOWING:
THE NUMBER SEVENS

In general, those with a seven-birth date are unusual people with special talents. Intellectual and absorbed, they are often considered loner and lover of solitude. They generally love nature, animals, and serene environments. Material success means less to them then being able to live life by their own rules. By nature they are deep peoples, intuitive and observant with spiritual and technical abilities. Seven are usually cautious and move very slowly when making decisions. Alcoholism is sometime a problem for sevens. They do not take advice well.

IF YOU WERE BORN ON THE 7th

You will succeed if you will learn to concentrate on one thing at a time. Your intuition will lead you to the right opportunities and then you have to get specialized training in the field you have chosen. You may have fine technical abilities. Your work may involve a great deal of research or you may be a farmer or a rancher, immersed in the land. Always follow your hunches rather than someone else advises. You should realize that you have strong opinion that you may not want to compromise, and relationships may suffer from your intractability. You will find your opportunities coming to you though patient waiting; if you try to be aggressive, you may experience frustration at the pace of events. Never gamble.

Your attitude of caution in regard to money is correct. You may play an esoteric instrument or have unusual hobbies and friends. You have an affinity for the country and animals, and meditation and solitude are absolute necessities for you. You may be prone to be quite and have few special friends rather than many.

IF YOU WERE BORN ON THE 16th

Yours is one of the most unusual birthday numbers. It brings startling events, which become turning point in your life. Your friends will be highly unusual. You may chosen an eccentric lifestyle and always have a feeling that you are somehow different. The 16 are a karmic number. This may mean that you have connections with people based on past life experiences and you will feel a special quality when you meet them-or by the way you meet them. Life is never dull with the 16. Many things are learned the hard way. You do not take undue risks. Your attitude may complicate your working or marital situations. Because of the nature slowness of the Sevens, you may procrastinate. You are analytic and may pursue technical or historical fields. You may uncover facts of great significance or invent something entirely new. You insist that friends be of high quality. You may love antiques and stamp collections.

IF YOU WERE BORN ON THE 25th

You are very intuitive and impressionable and must guard against emotional instability through the intensity of your emotion. You may be hard for others to understand.

You can be extremely talented in artistic or musical fields and have great rapport to animals. You may even choose to be a veterinarian. Three may be difficult times (especially around ages 27 and 28) when you will find some type of therapy valuable in assisting your personal growth. There may be a bisexual nature. Do not cut yourself off from family and friends when you are feeling melancholy. Find a stable diet and exercise routine.

IF YOU BORN ON THE 8. (EIGHTH) OR 17th (SEVENTEENTH), OR 26th (TWENTY SIXTH) OF ANY MONTH THAN KINDLY READ THE FOLLOWING:
THE NUMBER EIGHTS

In general, Eight are hardworking, practical people. They are never without a desire to better their position and posses a knack for knowing how to do it. They have a natural self-confidence and do not stay in subordinate position for long.

They are natural leaders and managers and, while their associates may admire them, are also somewhat feared. They are not usually considered "one of the gang". As women eight must acknowledge an ability to direct and achieve. Eight knows the power value and mechanic of money by second nature. They may be strict, but are always fair and loyal to those who serve them. They may appear somewhat formal. They are dependable, objective, and dominant.

IF YOU WERE BORN ON THE 8th

You are very ambitious person, highly motivated to do well. You will stop at nothing to move forward to your chosen work. You need a career of business that will challenge you. You will not stay in a subordinate role, but will rise to the level of supervisor, manager, foreman, head of department, or professional very quickly usually through your own hard work unaided by "lucky breaks". Women who were born on the 8th need to work outside the home. Eight will find the success in any large structured organization, such as factories, law firm, criminal justice system, military, financial institution, hospital or government. In business, you should be your own boss. You have a way with money and will do very well in life. When success evades you, you have a tendency to become cynical or bitter. You are serious and mature, discipline and competent.

You may have trouble sharing your emotional side with the opposite sex; as a woman you may seem very independent and dominant to men. Eight need a partner who is willing to differ them. You buy only name brands.

IF YOU WERE BORN ON THE 17th

You are dynamic go-getter. You have the daring and courage to undertake large projects and the executive ability to delegate to the right people. You have one of the best business and financial outlook possible. Your business may be at the cutting edge of its industry.

You have vision and determination-unbeatable qualities. If you are male, opposite sex will be highly attracted to your power. If female, you will instill admiration in others, although you may need to emphasize your feminine qualities to attract men.

The number should attain the highest achievement; integrity is the key. Your judgment is nearly infallible and you are outstanding trouble-shooter. Do not get bogged down with details delegate! You admire scholars and historians and will excel in technical, factual writing. You are never vague.

IF YOU WERE BORN ON THE 26th

You are much less intense then the 17. You have a strong emotional capacity and love nature. Harmony is very important to you. You will be oriented towards marriage as much as work. You love to dress well, have a fine house, and well brought up children (for which you take credit). You are the more generous Eight. You may brood about the past, hanging on to old arguments and beliefs. You may have big ideas, but want to include others to help you, as you may not be as self-confident as the other Eight. You are more introspective and psychologically analytic. You might consider a catering business, diplomacy, or administrative work in the social science.

IF YOU BORN ON THE 9. (NINTH) OR 18th (EIGHTEENTH), OR 27th (TWENTY SEVEN) OF ANY MONTH THAN KINDLY READ THE FOLLOWING:
THE NUMBER NINES

In general, nine are broad minded, idealistic, generous loving people with multiple talents.

They are interested in universal good and often go into fields where there is broad scope. Music, Art, drama, healing arts, the ministry, metaphysics, social reform any area is open to them. They have a strong need to express the self, but not necessarily in the more ego-cantered way of the One or Eight. Nines can be diffused and vague. They are very vulnerable to outside influences and often experience difficulty in deciding what they are going to be or in making decision in general.

Young Nines may choose an eccentric life style to rebel against tradition. They may or may not continue on that path depending on who they meet and the experiences that influence them. Nines need to learn not to take everything personally. They will take up causes and wonder why others are not so involved as they are. They will do well in groups that strive to reform and educate. All nines have dramatic style whether in their dress, speech, manner, or philosophy. They can be distant and cool.

IF YOU WERE BORN ON THE 9th

You can succeed in any artistic, healing, teaching, philanthropic, or musical line of work. You are idealistic and emotional. Life is serious for you and you feel such a need to be of service to the world that you have trouble making up your mind about which carrier you follow. You are very capable but have some trouble concentrating on everyday details. You become absorbed in whatever interests you and you have many interests. You may have a metaphysical outlook towards world problems. You will find yourself involved with much group work throughout your middle years. You may travel extensively and your life will always be full of surprises. You may be drawn to transformational work through therapy.

IF YOU WERE BORN ON THE 18th

You can accomplish very great things when you put your mind to it. You have the drive and ambition of the one and the executive capacity of the Eight. You will have to push yourself a bit to get through the obstacles that will force you to acquire more knowledge and understanding. As a child you may have displayed a nature kind of maturity. You will not like to take advice from others.

Your own critical power are good and could be used professionally (especially in drama, art. And music). You definitely need to work the good for others.

IF YOU WERE BORN ON THE 27th

You are quieter then other Nines, but a keen observer of life. You may have musical or artistic ability and will yearn for distant places; you enjoy the poetry of the East, perhaps wish to be a member of an eastern religious community.

You would make an excellent journalist, wild life photographer, calligrapher, or antique dealer. The Nines has many talents and interests, which cam takes a while to find. You are generous and forgiving of friends. To be happy and fulfilled, you need to have an ideal to follow. You are always learning about letting go.

CHAPTER EIGHTEEN

REMEDIES ACCORDING TO LAL KITAB

The general remedies for different planets according to Lal Kitab are following: -

Remedies for Sun

1 Fast on Sunday.
2 Reciting or listening to Harivansha Purana.
3 Wheat, jaggery and copper etc, to be given in charity.
4 Maintaining good moral characters.
5 Wearing Ruby or in place of Ruby copper can be used.
6 Throwing copper coins in the flowing water.
7 Keep main entrance from east.
8 Keeping away from black marketing and black marketers.
9 Do not give in alms the article pertaining to Sun if Sun is exalted.
10 Service of Government officials.

Remedies for Moon

1 Keep fast on Monday.
2 Worship Lord Shiva or go on pilgrimage to Amaranth.
3 Milk, rice or silver to be given in alms.
4 Wear a white milky pearl or alternatively silver can be substituted.

5 Blessings of mother (grand mother, mother-in-law, mother's mother, mother's sister).
6 Silver nails in the feet of the bed.
7 Silver or rice to be dropped in the Crematorium.
8 Taking bath in the Ganges or running water.
9 water tank overheads should be cleaned in 5 to 6 months.
10 No water pump or well under the roof.
11 Giving things pertaining to Moon in charity if Moon is in debility but not when she is in exaltation.

Remedies for Venus

1 Fast on Friday.
2 Desi ghee, curd, camphor etc. to be given to places of worship.
3 Wear diamond or the pearl.
4 Perfuming the clothes and using cream & face powder etc.
5 Clothes should be clean and ironed.
6 Worn out clothes or burnt clothes should never be worn.

Remedies for Mars

1 Fast on Tuesday.
2 Sindoor to Lord Hanuman.
3 Throw in the running water pulse of masoor, or honey or sindoor.
4 Service of brother.
5 Sleeping on deerskin.
6 Pure silver to be used.

Remedies for Mercury

1 fasting on Wednesday.

2   Green things in alms or dropped in the running water.
3   Copper coin with a hole to be dropped in the running water.
4   Service of domesticating goat and parrot.
5   Belt to be used.
6   Bangles and clothes of green colour to be given to eunuchs.
7   If Mercury is in debility the things of Mercury should be given in alms, but never should this be done when Mercury is in exaltation.
8   Blessing of daughter, sister, and father's sister, mother's sister and wife's sister. They should also be helped to the extent possible.

Remedies for Saturn: -

1   Fastings on Saturdays.
2   Bhairon worship and giving wine to him in temple of Bhairon.
3   Milk for the serpents.
4   Oil and wine to be distributed free.
5   Loaf of bread with mustard oil on it to be given to dogs and cows.

Remedies for Rahu: -

1   Sarawati Poojan.
2   Never accept electrical items, steel vessels or blue clothes.
3   Kanya dan.
4   Wearing Gomed.
5   live in joint family.
6   Never use tobacco.

Remedies for Ketu:-

1 Fasting on Ganesha Chaturthi and Ganesha Poojan.
2 Til, lime and Bananas etc. to be given in charity.
3 White and black pet dog in the house or feeding such a dog daily.
4 Good moral character and conduct.
5 Sour things to be given to female children below the age of nine years.
6 Black and white till to be dropped in running water.

CHAPTER NINETEEN

KNOW ABOUT YOUR SELF THROUGH NUMEROLOGY

READ WHAT YOUR BIRTH NO HAS TO SAY ABOUT YOU
DOUBLE DIGITS NUMBERS
COMPOUND NUMBERS

A double-digit number or a compound number is s the mixture or combination of two single digit number and its characteristics are mostly dominated by that of a single digit number that it represents.

The dual number highlights certain aspects, of the two single digit numbers but it never eliminates any aspect completely. For example number ten highlights the leadership ability of a 1, number 30 is lead of 3, and a 60 is a high trend of number 6. A short explanation of double-digit numbers from number ten to number ninety nine are given below:

To find your dual digit number, let us take the total of the letters in your name before you reduce them to a single digit. The ultimate meaning of the double-digit numbers is given in detail:

Number 10 indicate all the qualities of that of number 1. It shows the person is powerful leader, sharply focused in his thoughts and nature and is Stream lined for success. This person can be ruthless in the persuasion of his aim and goals. He can become a dominating and angry tyrant.

Number 11: Highly intuitive, psychic, sub-conscious and the conscious mind, highly charged. can be at times neurotic.

Number 12 It is highly creative, individualistic, and unconventional. Represents the interests self-centered

Number 13: Hard work and slow progress, difficult but rewarding down-to-earth. Reliable, trustworthy, rigid and lacking a sense of humor.

Number 14: Wild streaks. Changing attitude and adventurous, capability to destroy, lack of focus and commitment, trouble shooter. Guard against self-indulgence.

Number 15: Loving, forgiving, and extremely tolerant, responsible, successful, dynamic, and strong. travel, adventure, and experimentation. This number can bring self-relent.

Number 16: Difficultly faced, especially during the early part of life. great potential, spiritual growth and self-knowledge. Self-destructive.

Number 17 It is spiritual growth, faith, and balance. It is also wealth or bankruptcy. It is an inner struggle to remain true to spiritual and moral values.

Number 18: Spiritual, International Business specialist, disparity between idealism and selfishness, lacking consciousness.

Number 19: Strong and individualistic. Self-reliant and confident, bring loneliness, qualities of a leader and bullish.

Number 20: Sensitive, intuitive, vulnerable to criticism, generates emotional problems weakness and cowardice in case of challenges.

Number:21 Procrastinate. Individualistic, and unconventional and intuitive.

Number:22 demanding and obsessive, living on edge. Progressive. Need to devote self to something larger than life.

Number 23: Unrealistic, surrendered, people lover, freedom fighter, a promoter of causes.

Number 24: domestic struggles and divorce, counsels and comforts others. It likes music, particularly rhythm.

Number 25: Spiritual leader. Lover of group endeavors. too serious. great difficulty in sharing feelings with others.

Number 26: Excellent in business and management. a good strategist, workaholic, often disorganized in personal affairs.

Number 27: Counselor, volunteer, an artist, successful, inheritance nature. rigid and narrow-minded.

Number 28: Ruthless, dominating and angry compassion and intolerance.

Number 29: high sensitivity, imaginative and creative powers, More serious and less social.

Number 30: Humorous, communication skill, creativity. jovial, superficial.

Number 31: more extrovert and fun-loving, more creative and unfaithful.

Number 32: moody, sensitive, up and down emotionally,

Number 33: Self-sacrifice, dependent, teacher. Comfort ability to other. and compulsive liar.

Number 34: intelligent. Spirituality and purity. Sharing with others, strong warrior.

Number 35: Freelancer, business adviser cum creative-- inventor, gadget-designer, socialite, but does not work well with others.

Number 36: Creativeness, genius. self-consciousness, inhibited, aloofness.

Number 37: individualistic, a scholar, a voracious reader, excellent imagination, often disorganized.

Number 38: more realistic. Very intuitive, not a good admitter, earning through sale of art or antiques. Generates phobias.

Number 39: Functional art. good in acting and dancing. Problems in rejection and separation.

Number 40: organized, systematic, and methodical. Critical of others, intolerant, and sometimes prejudicial.

Number 41: capable of directing energies to many different projects successfully. selfish, has a lack of humor, and is sometimes criminal.

Number 42: Insensitive, political aspirations. Administrator works in government institutions.

Number 43: Inferiority complex, good concentration, best perfectionism, frustrations, and feeling of inferiority.

Number 44: Good for business, military career a visional and a doer. Great potentiality.

Number 45 banking, or international institutions. Not comfortable with self. Cynical.

Number 46 It represents leadership (see 10), and is often tactless and rude. It is always well prepared and confident.

Number 47: inner struggle between practical, down to earth spiritual balancer, achiever, it is a prophet and counselor extraordinaire.

Number 48 a visionary planner. lost in unrealistic dreams.

Number 49: caretaker makes effort for others. Problem-solver. be a hero and a friend to everyone.

Number 50: A high octave of 5. Freedom-loving, versatile. Open to new ideas, willing to take a chance. Possess sexual hang-ups.

Number 51: It is more independent and aggressive.

Number 52 creative intuitive sensitive and clever.

Number 53 business-oriented. more verbal, creative, and intelligent

Number 54 less organized and disciplined, difficulty in finishing projects. Dreamer and idealistic.

Number 55 It is extremely freedom-loving, and likes to travel. social, selfish lonely. success in sales.

Number 56 extreme sensitivity, balance, a desire for freedom with an equally, strong desire to be part of a family

Number 57: intelligence inventiveness creative and unconventional wisdom late in life,.

Number 58: opinionated hard worker, successful. Opportunist, fine decision maker and dogmatic.

Number 59: very persuasive convincing. successful lawyers and fundraisers. uncanny ability with people diverse cultures.

Number 60: loving, caring, responsible. brings subservience.

Number 61: Problems in love relationships. In need of family and friends demanding, secretive; researchers, law officers,

Number 62: medical field less sensitive, caretaker.

Number 63: unfriendly, less outgoing. sexually promiscuous.

Number 64: un comfort ability un- organized and more creative.

Number 65: freedom and domestic affairs brings a criminal tendency.

Number 66: Generous to a fault, financial ups and downs. Loyal, loving. Successful in itself.

Number 67: analytical intelligence creativity. Inventors and mathematicians.

Number 68: Good in business, insensitive, very loyal. sense of humor.

Number 69: teachers, Creativeness, self-sacrificing activists medical professionalisms.

Number 70: loner, truth knowledge seeker Intelligence, originality. eccentric.

Number 71: less authoritative a loner.

Number 72: an excellent conversationalist, voracious reader.

Number 73: independent likes to work alone. demanding in relationships.

Number 74 bad eating habits and disorder, premonitions and intense dreams.

Number 75 more analytical and less creative.

Number 76 management or organization. turn ideas into reality. dogmatism and religious fanaticism.

Number 77 most intelligent and inventive of all numbers. It also represents spiritual wisdom.

Number 78 struggle between the spiritual and the material. make and lose fortunes.

Number 79 Political and spiritual leaders concern for mankind, be ruthless and self-righteous.

Number 80 good businessmen. In management personals in military, entrepreneurs, lack of independence. It is an extravert number.

Number 81 money-oriented. lacks spiritual understanding. brings violence.

Number 82 leadership and courage. survivor. lack of stability in marriage. never get married or get married many times.

Number 83 more business-oriented and less sensitive and vulnerable.

Number 84: Little less in organization and quite visionary.

Number 85: trendy and bullish nature. masculine in figure,

Number 86: more self-oriented. Irresponsible self-indulgent.

Number 87: practical good in money handling struggle spiritual and the material thoughts.

Number 88: contradictions. business, not good for relationships. It is insensitive.

Number 89: aristocrat much travel. difficult for a person to be alone, even for a short period of time.

Number 90 respected by many self-sacrificing and humble. positive nature. likes to be aloof,.

Number 91 success in career, creative fields, unable to handle huge money.

Number 92 great concern for mankind.

Number 93 creative, in architecture and landscaping. Non commitment

Number 94 practical humanitarian, not comfortable with travel, and dislikes changes.

Number 95 humanitarian, is impractical, dreamer. loves travel and change.

Number 96 loving nature self-sacrificing focused on community family, friends, and relations.

Number 97: sensitive. quiet worker and loves to read.

Number 98: idealist, shows emotions. not easily understood by others.

Number 99: artistic genius. often misunderstood, victim of gossip, brings jealousy possessiveness to relationships and friendship.

CHAPTER TWENTY

READ WHAT YOUR BIRTH NO HAS TO SAY ABOUT YOU

COMPATIBILITY WITH OTHER NUMBERS

Natives Ruled By Number 1

People born with various numbers, when we stand to applying numerology compatibility, us to find out who will be helpful to them in all their dealings. If you are born on 1st, 10th, 19th or 28th dates, your ruling number is 1. Natives who are governed by 1, with get help from people who are of 4, and 2 number persons of 7 as their number will also help them. Help and joint venture Differ In Numerology Compatibility. Please note help you from 8 persons will be good solid and long standing. There is no dispute or conflict with numerology compatibility for 1 and 8, But their marriage, love or joint venture in business, politics, or board meetings, will not be successful, as these persons will have opposite views on most matters and will not see eye to eye. Their vibrations oppose each other.

COMPATIBILITY

Natives Ruled By Number 2

If your birth day is 2nd, 11th, 20th or 29th, your number is 2. You will get help from natives ruled by 7. But people with 2 as number people are unreliable for you because, they may do you both good and bad. You can choose persons of 1, 3, 4, and 8, number person who will be help you and do good for you. If may become difficult for number 7 people to find out the right companion or partner for them for any help or assistance.

COMPATIBILITY

Natives Ruled By Number 3

If you are born on 3rd, 12th, 21st, or 30th. Your Number is 3. Persons ruled by 2 and 9 will be quite helpful. But you need to avoid people ruled by 5 and 6. You should also avoid Number 7 and Number 8 people They may not be helpful, fruitful and useful.

COMPATIBILITY

Natives Ruled By Number 4

If you are born on 4th, 13th, 22nd, or 31st, your Number is 4. You tend to get help is from persons whose have numbers 1 or 8. Slight help can be expected from the 4 and 2. But, from people with number 8 you will receive unexpected favors.

COMPATIBILITY

Natives Ruled By Number 5

If you are born on 5th, 14th, or 23th, your day number is 5. You seem to be the most fortunate and lucky person as compared to others. You ought to get help from all sides and corners. All the persons from 1 to 9, will be glad to help you.

COMPATIBILITY

Natives Ruled By Number 6

If you are born on 6th, 15th, or 24th your number is 6. As per symmetrical and multiple laws of numerology compatibility, you tend to get help from persons of 3, 6, and 9. You can expect to get excellent and extra ordinary help from number 3 natives also.

COMPATIBILITY

Natives Ruled By Number 7

If you are born on 7th, 16th, and 25th your number is 7. You would get help from natives ruled by 2, 7, 1, and 4. You can know your compatibility to your number with regards to the circle of your friends to know who comes under these numbers to assist you and help you in the event of crisis.

COMPATIBILITY

Natives Ruled By Number 8

If you are born on 8th, 17th, or 26th, you are ruled by number 8. You ought to get help only from the persons ruled by 1 and 4. You can also expect help from persons ruled by 8. But, this is a bit on lower side.

COMPATIBILITY

Natives Ruled By Number 9

If you are born on 9th, 18th, or 27th, your number is 9. Getting to apply numerology compatibility persons ruled by 3, 5, 6, and 9 would be helpful to you. But Persons ruled by 2 could harm you even if they try to assist and help you.

CHAPTER TWENTY ONE

NUMEROLOGY

Know About Your Self
Through Numerology
RELATIONSHIP

Relationship between Numbers, Alphabets and Planets,

In Numerology you can visualize a close Relationship between Numbers, Alphabets and Planets. The above all three shower immense vibrations. When these are in harmony, they are very lucky for you. Below is a Table of Numbers Alphabets and Planets. Each Planet vibrates in Harmony with its Number. And its Alphabets.

They are represented by these Numbers.

Planet	Number	Alphabet
Sun	1	A J S
Moon	2	B K T
Jupiter	3	C L U
Rahu, Uranus	4	D M V
Mercury	5	E N W
Venus	6	F O X
Ketu Neptune	7	G P Y
Saturn	8	H Q Z
Mars	9	I R

CHAPTER TWENTY TWO

KNOW ABOUT YOUR SELF THROUGH NUMEROLOGY

NUMEROLOGY AND PLANETS

Number Ruled by Planet
Sun

If you are born on the 1st, 10th, 19th, and 28th, of any month, the total when added of your birth number it becomes 1

You are ruled by Planet Sun.

It is said that you will be bold honest and straight forward and will order, control and influence all. You are strong diligent, and you work very hard to be successful. You are best situated for head of Religion, Political Leader, and good administrator.

This number also indicates that you can shine well in teaching astrology politics, medicine, and fine arts. You shy away from cheating and fraud and deceit. You would work hard to become a famous leader. At times you can become arrogant and proud and would blow your own trumpet, claim to be number one and often make false promises, and thus face failures. By this you generate enemies.

If you are a fairer sex or a lady, you appear to be more grown up. You may get eye sight and may need to wear spectaculars in life soon. After 45, you may be a victim of hyper tension or heart disease or some chest ailments.

NUMEROLOGY AND PLANETS

Number Ruled by Planet
MOON

If you are born on the 2nd, 11th, 20th, and 29th, of any month the total when added of your birth number becomes 2 you are ruled by the planet Moon.

This number ruled by moon influences your, thoughts, mind and imagination. Like water waves, you may have different moods of elevation and depression.

This tends to control your imagination, and allows you to become a great scholar. When your imagination runs out of control or amok, you seek to lose your head, and you wake up as a Lunatic or a mentally depressed person.

You could have a wavering temperament. In business, You toil and build the important toe or line of someone else than to work for your own profits. You find it to be an easy task to do this.

Since this planet Moon derives its light from the Sun. You too ought to shine in borrowed brightness and glory. As planet Moon do not show its one side to Earth. Similarly, you tend to hide your dark side from the public vision.

This planet shows that you are swayed by negative thoughts and suspicion. You show a rough exterior side to others. On the reverse side you are soft in your nature, like a cool glow of moon light. When someone becomes offensive against you, you are baffled and rattled. You try to compromise. But if someone is under your authority, you enslave them, terrorize them, and extract work from them.

At some point of time if some of your subordinate retaliates your emotions, you tend to become irritated and make you to surrender. This also makes you nurse fears about everyone and you do like to trust others. You like to do all by yourself. Numerology Meanings for No. 2 also reveal that, if you trust some persons, you fall for their flattery, and you get badly cheated. This is why, you have to be careful in your choice of friends. Assess well before choosing.

NUMEROLOGY AND PLANETS

Number Ruled by Planet
JUPITER

If you are born on the 3rd, 12th, 21st, and 30th, of any month, the total when added of your birth number becomes 3 you are ruled by the planet Jupiter.

In Numerology, number 3 stands for Jupiter. He is named as Guru of Devtas in Heaven. The planet Jupiter is also the Lord of signs Sagittarius and Pisces in the zodiac signs. Since planet Jupiter rules Number 3. It donates and signifies Wisdom Knowledge, Selflessness Sacrifice, and Service.

This number 3 and the planet ruling it makes you honest, hardworking and intelligent. You expect discipline from your colleagues and subordinates and also adhere to and obey your superiors implicitly. In spite being a tough exterior, you are not hard hearted. You only do what is reasonable for you and as per your conscience. You do not mind to help others, even without even thinking of any returns.

This number and the influence of this planet makes you orthodox. You follow your own culture and religion. You do not like to change your ways of life as per social norms. But you shy away from asking for help on the contrary you would like to help others. Your self-respect prevents you from doing that. This name umber and planet makes you good and great in nature and you may appear to be proud superficially. The name number also get you into altruistic deeds. You attain high positions in politics, by your own efforts and hard work. As such you are considered to be a lucky chap. If anything is to come to you it comes only after your sincere hard work.

This number imparts you rise and promotion only through gradual rise step by step. You would not t desire for anything which you cannot perform. You most of the time try to remain content with whatever comes to you in the course of your life, by sincere hard and honest work. With this ruling number, you are of two types. One with a good self-confidence, and the other without weak and timid. If you are the first type, you are bold, confident in what you do. You fight for what is right and justified, neglecting and unmindful of your oppositions. You have a self -scarifying nature and you would not mind scarifying for your country in the need of any crises and you would be ready to any suffering and personal loss.

Now if you happen to be of the second type, you would obey your elders and remain quiet. You work only for you and your family. Even if you do something good, you would justify yourself to be satisfied with a name, but may not get and publicity and become famous.

The added quality of this number is that it makes you the strong pillars of post in offices, institutions and in government departments. You would fill all the important government positions to serve officers, ministers and organizations. This number and planet also make you to shy away from earning a bad name. You stand for high regard and prestige. You are not interested to start or run a big institution. On the contrary you would like to work gladly for those who offer you good respect and service.

On the reverse side of it if your name number 3 gets weakened you turn out to be lazy, fond of vices gambling and do all unjust things. You become sensual, borrow funds, and fail to return, indulge in unlawful activities and even court imprisonment. Therefore, it is important to correct your name with positive vibrations of a new name by an expert.

NUMEROLOGY AND PLANETS

Number Ruled by Planet
RAHU

If you are born on the 4th, 13th, 22nd, or 31st. of any month, you are ruled by No. 4. You are ruled by Planet Rahu.

With this number and planet you become the a well-known person and people take you as a well-judged and well Informed person, well known, and a Source for Information, as a ready reckoner and an intelligent person.

You are a knowledgeable person who is fond of, collecting information about all walks of life and is always busy. You mostly represent a circle. You can cause changes in social circle, and your society. It is often your opinion which counts as the main public opinion.

Your name is well known in social circles. You are like and your name is on the lips of every one, as an authority, when somebody needs any information. You have the power of tongue to express, or gift of the gab or bridge. Your this number rules, your Intellect. You can cause and effect social revolutions. You make reformation and social changes by your speech and great literary writings. You are always seen busy talking to someone, or helping the others.

This makes you gather latest information on all subjects. You are the trusted source of information, on a wide range of subjects. We can see you in the street corners, restaurants, clubs and press meets. Your number represents the planet Earth. Its presiding lord is Ganesh.

Therefore, you happen to sharp and intelligent, soft spoken and pleasant. You are acquainted with almost everything and everyone. You have a wide range of friends. Your name makes you to be an authoritative person and your opinions cross others with the alternate views, If you are trying to be adamant, you also acquire secret enmity among your friend circles.

Also if you name and nature is in affliction you possess the power to change this nature well in time, to become amiable to all. You can win almost all friends and influence people. But you tend to keep only surface friendship with the oust, and maintain only a few close and sincere friends.

You are good in philosophy, literature, mythologies, research and religion. You keep on acquiring knowledge on a wider range of topics. This number makes you not so keen on becoming famous. You would like to fully enjoy life and are very much careful about your diet like your food and drinks. You are the one who asks for special medicines and tonics to improve your health.

On the positive side of it you are soft in nature. You are full of emotions and are easily hurt. But, you forget it quickly to get along well. Money does not come to you that easy.

You struggle for your earnings. But you enjoy spending money. You take pleasure in shopping for the latest gadgets in the and new electronics items in the market. You feel happy and get pleasure in keeping your house and drawing room very attractive.

You specially amaze your friends with your rare collections of different items. You are fond of games and you want to enjoy life to its fullest. During your old age, you do researches on Vedas, and philosophical literature. In your life, you think well, to indulge in those activities, which brings good wealth for you.

On the negative side of it your number is not considered and favored to be a good number and is often said that it is not good to have your name number as 4. If you have 4 as the day number and 8 as your life number, you will face lots of complications. It is always better for you to correct your name, by some expert fellow who can measure the vibrations of the number, and get the effect to a good change.

NUMEROLOGY AND PLANETS

Number Ruled by Planet
MERCURY

If you are born on the 5th, 14th, and 23rd, of any month, be sure that you are ruled by 5 and Planet is Mercury. You are ruled by Planet Mercury.

If you re ruled by No. 5 and planet Mercury you often take daring risks, consider nothing as impossible to achieve. Your Intellect works with tremendous Speed, and you become quite popular and successful in a short span of time. You quickly think of new methods and ideas, for which others take months. You work so well and often take the

lead for the rapid modern developments in our scientific life. You consider the whole world lags behind you. As you are fond of new business ventures and you do not get scared or are afraid of failures. You are lucky and successful and are liked by masses. Even If your day number is not 5 but your main number is 5, you start your life as per your day number; with the result you will be very popular in your later life. At times you can also be notorious, vagabond and non-reliable.

Your No. 5 gives you special powers of special attraction. Successful businessmen know this and change their business names to No. 5, in order to be successful. You can never fail. You fight back and win which makes you to constantly like changes and get into new enterprises. You are quite bored by routine.

Your spouse need to understand this secret of yours numerology. This number also ensures your business success. You can do any kind of business successfully. You think of quick tricky and novel ways of making money.

If you fail it becomes the stepping stone for your next big venture. You also like to earn well and spend well. If your this number is well placed in your birth chart and exalted, then, you achieve great name and fame. You perform miraculous and memorable things. You invent new ideas, new ways of marketing and new methods. Your number 5 warns that you have to be careful with your secrets. You simply cannot hide anything from others and this being your weakness you tend to lose all that is gained.

Your number five makes you easily to fall in love. It is instant love and out of passion rather than any reason. Changing everything is your passion and you love to change and this leads you to change your love quite often. You may end up in serious trouble for you.

Natives with ruling numbers 9, 18, and 27 attract you much. They would rule over you in the long run. Thus you need to make a wise choice. Persons ruled by No. 5, are not blessed to get children easily. If both husband and wife have the same number and are ruled by No. 5, then the question of issues is delayed or at times denied. It is better for them to try from early stages. If your this number happens to be afflicted you lead a life of telling lies by trickery and cheating others with false and fraudulent methods. You mishandle public funds. To avoid all this, you must correct your names with accurate vibrations by a good numerologist.

NUMEROLOGY AND PLANETS

Number Ruled by Planet
VENUS

If you are born on the 6th, 15th, and 24th, of any month, the total when added of your birth number becomes 6you are ruled by the planet Venus.

You would attain greatness in you gradually and this will transform your life to a status of comforts and luxury. No. 6 stands for Planet Venus this gives you an award to become are attractive, popular, and loved by all. This number will also make you to be fond of dance and music drama and theatre.

This loving number enriches you to dominate and rule over others. You would be surrounded by servants this will make you to lead a luxurious life. You tend to be gifted with name, fame, and riches. This number will also make you to love all attractive things. You will love beautiful things by nature and you will consider this life is to be fully enjoyable. You want to enjoy every moment and pleasure of your life. You possess a special quality to extract work from others in order to achieve your goals. And you work very hard, to make money.

This number and planetary influence makes you to become a great and good leader, and you would easily govern to rule experts, even though you do not have their knowledge.

You are helped by others to come up in your life. This also makes you excel in mantra, and all mystical sciences. You would get help from others, but you do not always reciprocate. You make false promises, and fail to keep them. You do not indulge in any superficial schemes and are always careful about your money and bank balance.

Number six makes you to give less and take more from others who serve you. Even if you make a go at others, there will be a money motive behind that. You will calculate profits and then only start anything. This number makes you to decorate your home with attractive things. And this makes you to spend money on costly and beautiful things. You love to be surrounded by opposite sex. Your love for ornaments and attraction for beauty makes you to lead a luxurious life.

You are a sweet-tongued person and by way of this nature you accumulate wealth using others method help and their talents, just to make your life look beautiful. Natives with 6 as their number are born lucky. They are very attractive, which makes others like you.

You are talented in your persistence and you achieve success. You would like to purchase success at any price thus you would enjoy others work and sacrifice. You are gifted with great riches and wealth. You tend live in a grand luxury.

If this number is in affliction it makes you to become a cheater. You cheat others very cunning and boldly. People known to you often get themselves cheated by you. You speak sweet and attractive words to delude and cheat them

This number when it is in powerful condition and the planet Venus influences you in a positive manner you enter the fields of medicine, religion, in all mystic sciences like mantras and Tantras and false remedies, about which yourself may not know anything. But you pretend to possess the a deep knowledge of everything. Thus you speak lies, to cheat others and make a living for yourself. You are not afraid of failures. You boldly try and try again to achieve great success

NUMEROLOGY AND PLANETS

Number Ruled by Planet
Ketu Neptune

If your are born on 7, 16, or 25 in any month, you are ruled by Number 7. total when added to your birth number it becomes 7 which indicates you are Ruled by Planet Ketu, Neptune

This number and planet makes you a saint a religious person and above all a philosopher. As far as your luck of natives of number seven is concerned, they lack to be lucky, in spite of their mental caliber and immense knowledge. If at all they become successful it is only after a lot of extreme hard work, struggle and hardships. Success eludes you in all your endeavors.

Many persons fail and end up doing small jobs and many others live with unfulfilled wishes desires and ambitions. Your ambitions tend to be more successful than your works of personal gain. You are bound to succeed, only if you work for others, than for your own profit.

The number seven persons have great powers of the mind and intellect. Since this number is ruled by Ketu which is a signification for wisdom. The 7 born are usually religious and inclined to be great thinkers and philosophers. On the positive side natives with number seven as their number are gifted with greater will power. Because of high mental energy, they talk less and speak in silence. However they can be good leaders but poor followers.

Such natives are often moody even with close persons. They easily become short tempered. Hence, they have few friends and do not properly enjoy their marital life. You tend to live separately or opt for divorce. The seven born fairer sex are seldom graced by beauty. Often their feminine charm is missing. They too find marriage bit difficult and feel unhappy in their married lives.

NUMEROLOGY AND PLANETS

Number Ruled by Planet
Ruled by SATURN
Saturn And No. 8

In Name Numerology, No. 8 stands for Planet Saturn total when added to your birth number it becomes 8 which indicates that you are ruled by Planet Saturn.

Be sure that you are ruled by number 8 if you face too many obstacles, often meet with accidents, Don't feel unlucky, it may be effect of Saturn. When this number is well placed in your birth chart or when it is exalted it makes you to become a saint, a religious follower. But if it happens to get afflicted, it makes you to commit crimes. Also if your Life number alone is 8, you will get the traits and qualities of No. 8 in due course of your life, and may undergo many sufferings your early days throughout your life. This number leads to you to face a lot of obstacles, which you may suffer from your childhood. You get small and little things, only after great struggles. You meet with many unexpected failures, accidents, and rejections. You would have too many risks even when you hold high positions.

When this gets into purity, you get the power to understand the scriptures. You are filled with compassion, love, and mercy. You sacrifice for the poor and the sick and will work for the down trodden. You spend your life in serving the poor and the sick. You get into religious teachings. You are eager to strike with God.

This number tends to makes you appear nice and clean. But from inside, you are see things with rage and thoughts of revenge. You revel in plans of rape fraud cheating, blackmails, murder and enter into the trade of counterfeit currencies. This also drives you to commit crimes and fill the prisons. But the same time, though you harbor such thoughts, but you lack the courage to do such acts. The planet Saturn that rules your number reveals that he stands for justice and administers it without fear or favor. He weighs your past deeds and punishes you and you get the deserved fruits accordingly.

These holy texts written on name numerology describe the bad luck of No. 8, but fails as how to escape from its evil effects. Intensive researchers have written that by changing names, the evil and bad effects for such persons are reduced to mere small events.

It has been said and told that if you modify your name number as to be 5 you would be buried from all evil effects of the bad planetary influence of this planet Saturn. Number 5 adds the power of good luck to you. Therefore, whatever are your sufferings with number 8, and if you have a proper name change in the tune and vibrations of No. 5, you are sure to escape from bad luck and ill effects. Hence with the help of an expert you need to change your name in the proper vibration of No. 5 that suits you.

NUMEROLOGY AND PLANETS

Number Ruled by Planet
Ruled by Mars
Mars and No. 9

If your number falls on the 9th, 18th, and 27th, of any month, you are ruled by 9 and Planet Mars. This number when added happens to be 9 you can confirm it that you are ruled by this number and planet only. Number nine is ruled by Mars.

Your number 9 is the highest in the series from 1 to 9. When multiplied to any number by this number 9, it bounces back to 9. And per this you will attain to the status as shown by 9 and if your number is single nine, you develop the qualities for 9 only. When you a fight for a cause, or rebel against an oppression, and fight for your country, you are ruled by Number nine.

You shine as a lawyer, chemist, doctor or a technician. This is the number that of a person born as a man who walks intelligently, on a road full of blood spots and stains, not seeing the danger below him. It tells you that your life is covered with dangers and accidents. This number also makes you a born fighter. You will everything without any fear and this makes you an embodiment of courage. This number fills your life with struggles. You happen to struggle with oppression, cruelty and authority and poverty. You would be fitted with the skills of the plumber, the machinist, the carpenter, the farmer, the doctor and the scientist or an engineer. You fight against the old and create a new order. You construct buildings, dams, and bridges. You also destroy them with bombs, in an emergency, or during war. You are the back bone of any civilization or any generation..

This number and planet generates love your country and are also in love your with your society which in turn makes you to help your fellow citizens. You would sacrifice everything for your nation. You also tend to fight for the rights and freedom of your fellow countrymen.

This number also makes you join the army, navy, or the air force. For most, you try to become a police officer. You like to handle the fire arms, machine guns, and bombs without any fear. You obey rules and you also demand obedience. You fight for your honor. You sacrifice your life for your country. You are blessed with sharp intellect. You appear cool in any crisis. You hide your feelings. But you plan secretly to defeat your enemies. You weigh all the pros and cons and strike to win and get it without much difficulty.

Many of you happen to become scholars and philosophers and intellectuals. This also makes you fit to become an intelligent leader and a good politician. When this number happens to be afflicted or is less lucky you tend betray your emotions and engage in quarrels. You generate enemies in this manner and waste your energy

If your number is affected by evils, it gives you a feeling of pride. You are charged with greed and jealousy. You brood on your weaknesses and on your enemies. You burst with anger. You become a nasty street fighter.

You are good at rare inventions. This fact gives you deep insights into chemistry and medicine. You exhibit your special powers, when your number is in exalting position. Be warned that you should not be polluted by bad associations of No. 2, 4, 7 or 8. When 9 is afflicted by your day number or name number, you are rude. You acquire bad traits and evil habits. When 9 is afflicted, you turn arrogant and commanding. You dictate terms. You are filled with lust. You get addicted to drugs and alcohol. You take pleasure in torturing and hurting others.

You can have your name organized and you should not have your name in Numbers matching the twos sevens or eights. If at all that is so in such situations, that you must correct your number 9 numerology by making your name vibrate in perfect harmony with your day and life numbers. Get it rectified and corrected by an expert numerologist, who can measure your name vibrations. Your number also attracts people to come forward to help you.

A single person like you will not make the most and you cannot be built without the helps from persons known to you and in your circle. You have people, all around and you only need to find them to succeed. Hence you need to apply your numerology compatibility to choose for best help and enlist their support you will succeed to be a winner.

CHAPTER TWENTY THREE

KNOW ABOUT YOUR SELF THROUGH NUMEROLOGY

READ WHAT YOUR BIRTH NO HAS TO SAY ABOUT YOU GEMS AND STONES FOR ALL NUMBERS

Gem Stone for No. 1

The best suited stone or gem according to numerology for number one is Ruby. It enhances your fortune or your luck powerfully. Alternately you can also use yellow sapphire and Topaz. These would help improve your health and give you success in your actions, deeds and in your life.

We could find that these gems, helps in promoting healthy growth in our young sons and daughters. As an grown up person, you could wear Ruby or yellow sapphire. Both are fine for you. You have to wear it in your right hand in ring finger made in gold ring.

Gem Stone for No. 2

The best suited stone or gem according to numerology for number two is Pearl. It enhances your fortune or your luck abundantly. Alternately you can also use Jade, Moon stone, and Tiger's Eye. These would help improve your health and give you success in your actions, deeds in your life.

All are fine for you. You have to wear it in your right hand in smallest finger made in silver ring. Jade has a particular medical use. It relieves your stomach disorders. The Tigers Eye is good for your children.

Gems for No. 3

The best suited stone or gem according to numerology for number three is Amethyst. Amethyst is of a violet color. There are many benefits. It enhances your luck abundantly. Alternately known for its anti-drunkenness properties, it greatly powers you up in your decisions.

It prevents you forever from becoming over intoxicated. These would help improve your health and give you success in your actions, deeds in your life. You can also use yellow sapphire with a golden hue. It is also highly favorable for you. It enhances your luck and worldly success. You must were your gem in your left hand, in your ring finger, studding it over gold.

Gems for no 4

The best suited stone or gem according to numerology for number Four is Garnet.. There are many benefits. It enhances your luck abundantly. The next choice is blue sapphire. Select it with the blue light color. Alternatively opal can also be used.

Gems for No. 5

The best suited stone or gem according to numerology for number Five is, Diamond. It should be highly of good quality and have the specification and be genuinely pure. It should be seen that it need to shine with the glow of the light. Zircon can be used as an alternate gem.

Gems for No. 6

The best suited stone or gem according to numerology for number six is Emerald. Circular or opal size structure should be taken. It powers mental strength, self-confidence, and immense happiness. It should be a flawless piece having some luster.

Gems for No.7

The best suited stone or gem according to numerology for number seven is Cat's Eye. There are many benefits. It enhances your fortune and makes you very strong.

Gems for Number 8

The best suited stone or gem according to numerology for number eight is Blue Sapphire. It can be tested, put a piece of blue sapphire in a glass of milk and if the there is a bluish layer than it is a good gem to be worn. High quality Sapphire showers good luck.

Gems for number 9

The best suited stone or gem according to numerology for number nine is Coral. It comes from the deep seas from the coral rocks, created by coral making insects. It removes blood related diseases and showers immense Luck. It gives you victory over your enemies. It bestows health and riches.

CHAPTER TWENTY FOUR

KNOW ABOUT YOUR SELF THROUGH NUMEROLOGY

READ WHAT YOUR BIRTH NO HAS TO SAY ABOUT YOU
The Letters of Your Name and Numerology
FOR ALL NUMBERS

When analyzing your own name, it's important to know that in Numerology, each letter in your name has a specific meaning and a number corresponding to it, and the influence that letter has on you. Someone who has changed the first vowel in their name for some reason, indicates a person who was uncomfortable and is now fine after changing his name letter to the compatibility of its number with his name. Here is a brief description as to what your name alphabets means in terms of numerology to you.

They are from A to Z we describe the same as follows:

The specific meaning of letter A in Your Name

You are a natural leader have some fine ambitious and a free thinking personality. If someone pressurizes you and makes you to change your mind you straight away oppose him

The specific meaning of letter B in Your Name

You are sensitive but still manage to be compassionate and personable and compassionate. In order to be happy you always desire to be at peace. Although you are very sincere and loyal, you seek to keep an open mind and think for yourself more often than others.

The specific meaning of letter C in Your Name

You have a strong instinct and you work whole heartedly in any project. You express yourself freely with the result you are also very outspoken and upbeat. You have a strong courage to face any eventuality.

The specific meaning of letter D in Your Name

You need not be too stubborn as you are master in of getting the things done. Your sense of determination is strong. You sparkle under pressure and can get things quickly. You are grounded and pragmatic.

The specific meaning of letter E in Your Name

You love to have freedom. You believe strongly in parting and outings. You are the one who cannot be easily fooled. You can see a situation from many different angles.

The specific meaning of letter F in Your Name

You are good host, self-sacrificing and very easy to get along with. Your warmness shows in how easily you're able to take on other peoples grieve. Be careful not to indulge in positions where you're not comfortable, and try not to let other people's worries and problems drag you down.

The specific meaning of letter G in Your Name

You are an active person with the caliber to make things happen. You have a strong vision, and this could help you financially in the long run. You need to stand on your feet, even though you prefer to be very organized. At times you may feel bit to psychic. You may even feel psychic sometimes.

The specific meaning of letter H in Your Name

You have a strong vision to manipulate, also tend to make a lot of money and lose it fast. You may be ok with it in the long run. Your creativity will help you well. You would prefer to be alone. You would like to spend more time in outings and parties rather than fighting with others.

The specific meaning of letter I in Your Name

You are a compassionate artistic and a creative person who feels things deeply and have a great eye for everything. Make sure you have a nice balance and have the correct direction otherwise you might suffer from depression.

The specific meaning of letter J in Your Name

J spells the meaning in you that you are a well-balanced person. You are all about balancing the scales. You make an extra ordinary friend and you do your to work hard and try your best to make sure everyone is happy and comfortable. You need to motivate yourself to tap into natural talents.

The specific meaning of letter K in Your Name

You are an entertainer and it all about enlightenment with you. You get motivated and rely heavily on your skill to make good decisions. You are also a force to be reckoned with. Be careful of excitement or depression, because you tend to be highly effected.

The specific meaning of letter L in Your Name

You are very brainy, and tend experience life. But you should not allow this experience to make you arrogant. You have the qualities to be kind-hearted, honest and generous. Though you are quite fond of travel, you should always be careful during times of excitement and depression. You must maintain and equal balance.

The specific meaning of letter M in Your Name

You are fond of doing excess work and possess a high quantity of energy, to do extra work and you don't need much rest or sleep and are very healthy. You also really like to be a homebody, however, and need a steady financial base in order to feel secure. Also make sure your drive doesn't make you impatient with other people.

The specific meaning of letter N in Your Name

You seem to be creative, original. You are also strong-willed and you have strong opinions to match with the people of your interest. You are organized in your life, with would like your share of romantic meetings.

The specific meaning of letter O in Your Name

Your moral is high and your spiritual believe is quite strong as is your will. You would like to make laws and rules, you are also sensitive and take all things very deeply. You must avoid being jealous might be a problem for you. Be careful not to and suspicious.

The specific meaning of letter P in Your Name

You are very intelligent possess immense knowledge, You are the center of attraction and People get great first impressions from you, but you can also seem keep distant from them. Although you have great sense to be patient but at times you can be extremely short tempered and impatient. Make sure to let this go, be more generous with the growing time.

The specific meaning of letter Q in Your Name

You are a magnet of collecting immense money, but your intolerance and instability can lead to financial downfalls. You are a born leader with a great power to preside, but on a personal level, you're a tough nut to crack. People find you mysterious and may gossip frequently about you.

The specific meaning of letter R in Your Name

You take things very strongly and you enrich the power of your but do not image it outwardly. You are work alcoholic and can do your job with high energy. You need to make sure to keep a balance and work well with others, even though you are prone to this nature.

The specific meaning of letter S in Your Name

You need to make sure that you are taking every decision very carefully. You being real charmer, a sense of warmth and devotion is being inherited but this can lead to overly dramatic situations and you may be confronted with many emotional ups and downs.

The specific meaning of letter T in Your Name

As you are in often seen tackling with new and exciting projects. You would like to move in fast lane but you must be reminded by yourself to slow down at bit. Being aggressive in your relationships you appearance should be in check, and not too sensitive.

The specific meaning of letter U in Your Name

You are prone to a policy of give and take and would like to lead this kind of life. You might gain a lot, only to lose it, but neither less will always break even. Power yourself to think faster on your feet and then commit wholeheartedly to involved with anything. You need to guide your instinct and creativity. You look glamorous in awkward situations too will show your positive temperament.

The specific meaning of letter V in Your Name

You are a pillar and you have great intuition. At times you may even feel bit psychic. Having a strong imagination, it may be hard to separate fact from fiction. You have high aimed goals and the will to bring them into reality. Use your efficiency, but be careful not to be too centered, there lies the real danger.

The specific meaning of letter W in Your Name

You think from your inner heart and you have a great sense of a purpose. You being an active person, you like to be involved in as many activities. Your mystical magic means you surround yourself with interesting people, because you have the powers of excellent conversation. You are advised to take full advantage of your own creative.

The specific meaning of letter X in Your Name

You have the quality of being creative, sensual person who mix up with people easily and gathers important information like a sponge. Be careful that this enthusiasm and passion doesn't make you too passionate in sexual matters. You can also be moody and have to be careful to avoid addictions.

The specific meaning of letter Y in Your Name

You come across to be self-reserved person even though you may love to be free and your ambition and courage make you naturally independent, even though. You need to avoid being too slow in making decisions or else you would lose all the profits that you have gained.

The specific meaning of letter Z in Your Name

You possess magical and mystical and you usual take the sunny side of the street, to say that you have high standards of living. You balance this out with common sense and understanding. You are wise and quick on your feet, but should not to be impatient or impulsive.

CHAPTER TWENTY FIVE

KNOW ABOUT YOUR SELF THROUGH NUMEROLOGY

READ WHAT YOUR BIRTH NO HAS TO SAY ABOUT YOU
BRIEF DISCRIPTION OF YOUR
NUMBERS FOR ALL NUMBERS

Number 1 - Initiative, independence, forcefulness (a masculine number).

Number 2 - Tact, diplomacy, attention to details (a feminine number).

Number 3 - Self-expression, ambition, spirituality, luck, easy success.

Number 4 - Labor, material, routine work - little paid compensation, unlucky.

Number 5 - Inventive genius, imagination, charm, restlessness, adventurous.

Number 6 - Tenacity, conscientiousness, achievement by working with others, domestic.

Number 7 - Mysticism, isolation, poets and dreamers; misunderstood by co-workers or companions.

Number 8 - Reason, judgment, financial success, organization.

Number 9 - Sympathy, generosity, dramatic, artistic talent (higher octave - teacher, master).

Planets and Numbers

There are many Planets in our System on which all calculations are based. Each planet rules a particular sign and has individual characteristic, vibration, trait that influences the person born under it. Each planet is given a number. The Nine Planets, with Corresponding Numbers and, their Zodiac signs are:

The sun and the moon are the only two planets having 'double numbers'. The sun and Uranus are interrelated and so is the moon and Neptune. There is a strong attraction between numbers 1-4 and 2-7 and these four numbers are compatible with each other.

Numbers 7 and 4 were allotted to the moon and the sun until Neptune and Uranus were discovered. Presently, number 4 is the number of planet Uranus or Rahu

PLANET RULES	NUMBER	ZODIAC SIGNs
Mars	9	Aries
Venus	6	Taurus
Mercury	5	Gemini
Moon	2, 7	Cancer
Sun	1, 4	Leo
Mercury	5	Virgo
Venus	6	Libra

Mars	9	Scorpio
Jupiter	3	Sagittarius
Saturn	8	Capricorn Aquarius
Jupiter	3	Pisces

.... THE .... END ....

OUR OTHER PUBLICATIONS
ARE ON SALE

"MICROSCOPY OF ASTROLOGY"
"MICROSCOPY OF NUMEROLOGY"
"MICROSCOPY OF REMEDIES"
ORDERS FOR BOOKS CAN BE PLACED AT:
orders.india@partridgepublishing.com
channelsales@authorsolutions.com
AND AT OUR CONTACT ADDRESS:
PLEASE SEND YOUR QUERIES TO:
BALDEV BHATIA
CONSULTANT-NUMEROLOGY-ASTROLOGY
C-63, FIRST FLOOR
MALVIYA NAGAR
NEW DELHI-110017
INDIA
TEL NO 919810075249
TEL NO 91 11 26686856
TEL NO 91 7503280786
TEL NO 91 7702735880
MAIL US AT: baldevbhatia@yahoo.com
OUR MOST SOUGHT WEB SITES:
HTTP://WWW.ASTROLOGYBB.COM
HTTP://WWW.BBASTROLOGY.COM
HTTP://WWW.BALDEVBHATIA.COM
HTTP://WWW.BALDEVBHATIA.US
HTTP://WWW.BALDEVBHATIA.ORG
HTTP://WWW.BALDEVBHATIA.INFO
HTTP://WWW.BALDEVBHATIA.NET
HTTP://WWW.BALDEVBHATIA.BIZ
HTTP://WWW.BALDEVBHATIA.IN
HTTP://WWW.MICROSCOPYOFASTROLOGY.COM

Special Note

FROM THE AUTHOR BALDEV BHATIA

THANK YOU FOR READING MY BOOK

MY SINCERE PRAYERS

FOR ALL MY READERS

"GOD BLESS YOU ALL"

"ANY ONE WHO READS AND KEEPS THIS BOOK AS HOLY MANUSCRIPT, GOD IS SURE TO BLESS HIM/HER, WITH ALL THE PEACE, HAPPINESS, WEALTH, HEALTH AND PROSPERITY OF THIS UNIVERSE"

Baldev Bhatia

Author